THE SHITSHOW

ALSO BY THESE AUTHORS

Is It Just Me or Is Everything Shit?:
The Encyclopedia of Modern Life

Is It Just Me or Is Everything Shit?: Volume Two

The Best of Is It Just Me or Is Everything Shit?

Blighty: The Quest for Britishness, Britain, Britons,
Britishness and the British

Is It Just Me or Has the Shit Hit the Fan?: Your Hilarious
New Guide to Unremitting Global Misery

Sorry, But Has There Been a Coup?

The Shape of Shit to Come

THE SHITSHOW

AN 'IS IT JUST ME OR IS EVERYTHING SHIT?' SPECIAL

Steve Lowe and Alan McArthur

sphere

SPHERE

First published in Great Britain in 2019 by Sphere

1 3 5 7 9 10 8 6 4 2

All characters and events in this publication, other than those clearly in the public domain, are fictitious and any resemblance to real persons, living or dead, is purely coincidental.

A CIP catalogue record for this book is available from the British Library.

ISBN 978-0-7515-7921-5

Typeset in Palatino by M Rules
Printed and bound in Great Britain by Clays Ltd, Elcograf S.p.A.

Papers used by Sphere are from well-managed forests and other responsible sources.

Sphere
An imprint of
Little, Brown Book Group
Carmelite House
50 Victoria Embankment
London EC4Y 0DZ

An Hachette UK Company
www.hachette.co.uk

www.littlebrown.co.uk

CONTENTS

THE SHITSHOW

INTRODUCTION

Why now? Why revisit the world's shitness now? To be honest, if you need to ask that question you're probably looking at the wrong book here, but let's indulge you. For fuck's sake.

In a word: Boris Johnson.

Okay, that's two words.

And also: Identity. Everyone's talking about it. Which is another five words.

So that's seven words altogether. You knew that. Moreover: the collective identity embodied in the increasingly tall tale of Jamie Oliver.

When the original *Is It Just Me or Is Everything Shit?* came out in 2005, the book established, through forensic investigative analysis worthy of Woodward and Bernstein or classic *Panorama,* that popular media personality of the era Boris Johnson was also, it transpired, an ambitious Tory politician. Who knew?

Jamie, meanwhile, had been plucked off the mean streets – well, the kitchen of the River Café (ask your gran) – to become a popular geezer TV chef. He wanted to feed the children. We should all feed the children. Actually, that sounds weird. We should all want the children to be fed. We don't desire to proffer them food ourselves. Look, as long as they get the food and it's all above board, then good.

Is It Just Me ...? was about different shit times. Ostensibly boom times. Are booms better than busts? Yes. But not when everyone's mining anything of value for booty – and just kind of shoddying up the world and privatising the fuck out of everything – while pretending the boom will never end. Boom and bust were no more, they said. The arseholes.

By the time of *Is It Just Me or Has the Shit Hit the Fan?* in 2009, sadly, and entirely unpredictably (ha!), the crash had arrived. On skates. Like everyone, Jamie, now a restaurant emperor, was feeling the pinch – the icy pinch of debt. 'There's been a lot of borrowing going on, mate,' he said. He wasn't feeling the icy pinch as much as people who weren't as loaded as him, but still.

When the leaders of the G20 nations (totalling, er, 24 nations) gathered in London to bail out the world economy, there could only be one choice of caterer ... But Gregg's were busy, apparently, so Jamie did it. Have you ever served finger food to a world leader? Jamie has. Sorry – that also sounds wrong in the current climate. He did some cooking for world leaders, all right? Christ, even 'laid on a spread' sounds like the sort of thing you 'can't say any more'.

Boris, meanwhile, was that year cast in *EastEnders* as the character 'Mayor of London', and, for his second job, was the Mayor of London – a city that is, depending on your point of view, either one of the world's very greatest cities *or* a massive nest of wankers. A tape emerged that year of him offering to provide the address of a journalist to an old pal so he could have the shit kicked out of said journalist.

And where is Jamie now, in the Trump and Brexit era, the era of rancour and confused identity, and rancour?

You've heard of Jamie's Italian? Of course you have. You didn't actually go there, clearly – at least, not often – but you're aware of it going belly up. But what of Jamie himself?

Jamie has gone back to Essex, from whence he came, looking for himself. Jamie is in flux. Aren't we all? He has taken up residence at the end of Southend Pier, in a confused Brexit town, hovering above contested fishing waters. All that is left of his previous empire is an internet show, put up on YouTube for free, called *Jamie and Jimmy's Friday Night Vlog*, in which Jamie and a loyal childhood friend sit about making endless cups of tea, dreaming about cooking for celebrities and changing the world with crusading campaigns, just like the old days. (See the entry: *Is Jamie Oliver now more metaphor than man?*)

Whatever did happen to Boris Johnson, though?

Lorraine Kelly: a philosophical disquisition on the nature of reality

Is she? Are we? Who is? And where are they? And how long will they be there? Does the Universe even exist?

These are the sort of essential philosophical questions latterly raised by Lorraine Kelly. Yes, the chatty Scottish lady off of the telly. That Lorraine Kelly (so-called).

But is 'that' 'Lorraine Kelly' 'the' 'real' 'Lorraine' 'Kelly'? No. In 2019 Lorraine Kelly established in court that the TV Lorraine Kelly and the 'real' Lorraine Kelly are not, in fact, the same person – and thus Lorraine the person did not have to pay a £1.2m tax bill from HMRC for monies paid for the services of 'Lorraine' the construct. Yes, it had been her on the telly. But also, it hadn't.

What is 'real', anyway? That is the question Lorraine Kelly has posed to humanity. And the taxman.

Summing up, Judge Jennifer Dean said: 'We did not accept that Ms Kelly simply appeared as herself – we were satisfied that Ms Kelly presents a persona of herself . . .

'Quite simply put, the programmes are entertaining, Ms Kelly is entertaining [big fan, Judge Jennifer Dean – big fan] and the "DNA" [of the programmes] is the personality, performance, the "Lorraine Kelly" brand that is brought to the programmes.'

This gets you thinking. What is this so-called HMRC? All those letters they send. Are they real? And those so-called deadlines ... maybe all these concepts, and indeed all concepts, are essentially plastic in nature.

Lorraine (or should that be 'Lorraine') fan Judge Dean went on: 'We should make clear we do not doubt that Ms Kelly is an entertaining lady [I'm not saying Judge Jennifer Dean watches *Lorraine* on her phone in court. I'm not saying that] [she does, though] [possibly], but the point is that for the time Ms Kelly is contracted to perform live on air she is public "Lorraine Kelly".

'She may not like the guest she interviews, she may not like the food she eats, she may not like the film she viewed but that is where the performance lies.'

Maybe everything is slipping. Is she even Scottish? Am *I* Scottish? I don't think I am. Am I Lorraine? Are *you* Lorraine?

I wrote to Eamonn Holmes to ask him if he is real. I did not get a reply, from which I conclude that Eamonn Holmes is not real.

Men's men of Brexit

Brexit is musk to men. Men's men. Maybe it's all that talk of sailing the seas, furiously trading (and perhaps a spot of light piracy? who knows?), and white-knuckle no-deals.

The Tory Party and the British Right in general have, of course, never been short of hardmen – never mind the

Duke of Wellington, even Tory wet and arch-Remainer Michael Heseltine once strangled a savage dog to within a whisker of death with his bare hands (his *mum's* dog! It had to be put down the next day!) – but the bearpit of Brexit has allowed some proper blokes to step up to the plate and roar . . .

David Davis. Alan Clark (randy Tory man's man) spotted Davis's talent early on, when the SAS part-timer scaled the walls of Clark's medieval castle as an after-dinner dare, strolling around the crumbling ramparts with his hands in his pockets (all these things are true). Spent his time as Brexit Secretary mastering Sudoku, re-reading Sven Hassel novels and (ironically) learning Spanish: *olé*!

Mark Francois. 'The pit bull terrier of the Brexit movement' (Nigel Farage): apparently that's a compliment. The vice chair of the European Research Group hit the headlines back in the expenses scandal days (ahh, remember those days?) for bloke-snack claims – Mars, Twiglets, Pot Noodles, *Peperami (!)* – that only just stopped short of a large doner (lamb, *not* chicken). Ripped up an anti-Brexit letter from the CEO of Airbus on live TV, stopping just short of calling him 'a fucking Boche'. Then, just before May's fall, he turned to the press gallery during PMQs, shaking his head and running his finger across his throat like a knife – which seemed a bit much, given the daily death threats to female MPs. Twiglets, though: man's food.

Johnny Mercer. Seems like a fictional character, but isn't. The Tory MP, who was in the Army, thinks welfare makes The Kids soft and that they should join the Army, like he did. When first elected in 2015, he spent three nights a week in his motor cruiser rather than claim expenses while attending Parliament (he probably survived by eating foxes). So far, so ex-military Toryboy. But Mercer simply refuses to exhibit character consistency. Never keen to dwell on his past in the military (ha!), Mercer also once did an advert for Dove, showering in the buff (you don't see Little Johnny, though). A winning contestant on *Celebrity Hunted,* Mercer also made an unexpected bid to become a Modernist poet with one particular article on Brexit: 'The sands are shifting beneath our feet . . . like a runaway horse.' What will he get up to next? Apart from mentioning he was in the Army.

Iain Duncan Smith. 'Theresa, Theresa, Theresa! Out, out, out!' That was him. IDS loves telling shit Tory leaders to go. Even used to shout at himself in the mirror, back when he was 'the quiet man' man's man. Another military chap of course. Invented Universal Credit: a benefits system that exacerbated a 'hunger crisis', according to Human Rights Watch. The Institute for Government (who *support* the idea of Universal Credit) said that 'the overall effect has been to plunge people already on low incomes into rent arrears and debt and in some cases homelessness'. Brutal!

Dominic Raab. Karate. Boxing. Ripped. Could fuck you up. Not taking any nonsense from uppity birds, calling feminists 'some of the most obnoxious bigots'. He backtracked slightly when photographed with his wife in their (her) kitchen for an article on his leadership ambitions. 'Is she a feminist?' he was asked. 'Is who a feminist?' he answered.

Tommy Robinson. Definitely hard as he hangs about with football hooligans. Sorry, Football Lads. The Democratic Football Lads Alliance. Yes, they like football. Yes, they're lads. But at heart they're just soccer-mad blokes' blokes who happen to like hanging out together in a large group, or alliance, as they love democracy. And aren't keen on Muslims.

Nigel Farage. Once called himself 'older women's crumpet' (sorry). On a side note, Nigel – you don't get to label *yourself* crumpet. That's not how it works. Often talks about his 'big vision' for Britain and his 'big message' for Westminster. All right man, we get it! In July 2019, urged beta Tory MPs to 'step aside' to let his Brexit Party beat Labour (to a pulp, in the car park).

Sajid Javid. Inspirational proof that people from Muslim backgrounds have an equal right, and an equal ability, to be complete arseholes. So tough he claimed to have grown up on 'Britain's hardest street' (in Bristol). Like hosting Britain's hardest pub, this is a claim made by all towns in Britain. 'Largest roundabout in Europe, mate' – that's another one.

Jeremy Hunt. Ha! Not really. Oft-referred-to during the Tory leadership contest as 'the richest man in the Cabinet': yes, but is he happy?

Stephen Yaxley-Lennon. (So hard they named him twice.)

Gavin Williamson. As Defence Secretary, sort of casually declared war. Well, wars. That's right, he declared wars. (Russia? China? Who wants some ... ?) Sacked for leaking state secrets (but he swears he never), he was very soon back in the affray as campaign manager for Boris Johnson's leadership bid. Allegedly used strongarm tactics such as making MPs who said they would vote for Johnson in the secret ballot(s) provide photographic evidence of their ballot paper with the 'X' duly scratched in the right box. He doesn't look that hard, I'll give you that: but they do say it's the quiet ones you need to watch. And the really big ones.

Steve Baker. On television actually said the words: 'Everyone knows I'm Brexit hardman Steve Baker.' And then, again on television, he started crying. Was he crying about his old mum, how she brought them all up on her own? No, it was in a Brexit documentary, talking about how difficult it was to vote against May's deal for the third time, when lesser men (Boris Johnson, Rees-Mogg, IDS ...) were caving like knaves and cowards. It's okay, mate, let it all out ...

Reviews for items on supermarket delivery sites: an important consideration

Peas might seem like small things. I mean, they *are* small things. But are they any less worthy of proper consideration for all that? If you can't take the little things seriously, are you a serious person? No, you are not a serious person.

Basically, whenever I'm eating peas, which I often am, I ponder, quite reasonably: yes, these peas are good, but are they good *enough*? Even when I'm enjoying my peas, there are suspicions that better peas are out there, somewhere, waiting. I mean, the term 'existential crisis' is over-used, but …

So I looked into peas. Someone has to. Where is *Which?* when you need it? Obsessively testing washing machines I expect, the endless cycle of washing cycles. So I decided to consult the hive mind …

Over at Sainsbury's, I read some positive reports about their own-brand Garden Peas:

'4/5 – I always keep these in the freezer. I have bought petits pois in the past but these are just as tasty and so handy for adding to stews, etc.'

Good idea about the freezer. I'll definitely bear that in mind. And the stews. But mention of petits pois got me thinking: should I be considering the smaller pea? Turns out the whole petit pois field is a minefield:

'1/5 – Worst frozen peas I can remember having. Nothing like the texture and flavour of petits pois, also they looked like full-size peas.'

Clicking on other brands, I discovered the scale issue was alarmingly widespread. What's going on here? Petits pois only have to be petit and pois. If they're just pois, that's pisspoor petits pois! I do like pois, but not if they're phoney petits pois, plain old pois masquerading as petits pois. It isn't right.

Over at Asda, *their* own-brand British Garden Peas were also receiving some mixed responses:

'2/5 – Disappointing – It should be 2½ minutes in my zapper but no matter what time I put them in for they come out mostly tough.'

Tough peas! That sounds like a phrase: tough peas. Tough peas, I'm afraid. That's just your tough peas! Go and tough pea yourself. I had to wonder, though: do these peas *never* go soft? Truly? I mean, that in itself would be kind of extraordinary. Others, however, find that these peas *do* go soft and *do* in fact make for some very satisfying pea-eating experiences:

'4/5 Fab – Just as good as the other makes. Love them and I love peas so I should know!'

Which sounds promising. After all, you do want your peas to be reviewed by pea lovers – albeit discerning ones, not people who simply love *all peas*. Maybe the other reviewer just didn't like peas?

Another poor review noted some inconsistency in the stock: '2/5 I bought a bag of these a few weeks ago and was amazed how beautiful they were . . .'

Amazed? By how beautiful they were? Respect is due.

We're definitely dealing with someone who can appreciate a pea there, and beauty. But it's still so contradictory! I needed some consistency, some cohesion. So I went to Ocado – I know it's decadent, but sometimes only the over-priced pea will do. But even here, checking out the reviews for their own-brand Petits Pois, I found the same extreme responses, to peas:

'1/5 I didn't think that it was possible to dislike peas but these petits pois are revolting. They taste revolting, they are hard and just plain horrible!'

So even at Ocado (Ocado!), pea hardness is an issue. What is going on? Then I thought: maybe this reviewer didn't know that frozen peas need to be cooked? We've all made that mistake when we're starting out. Then I was momentarily swayed back in the other direction by this opinion:

'5/5 Lovely and sweet. Only peas my son will eat . . .'

Which even rhymes – perhaps unintentionally, perhaps not. But *then* I started thinking about how many pea types this boy – or, who knows, *man*? – had to taste before hitting on this particular variety: 'Not these ones . . . no, not these, either . . . we must keep going, Mother . . . we *will* find them!'

And what could have been so very much amiss with all those other peas? Was I wrong to embark on this journey of discovery? Still the questions came. Even worse than before! Why this pea? Why not that pea? *La nausée!!! La nausée!!!* At this point, I just thought: I can't deal with all this any more, I'm not even going to buy *any* peas, you know?

Maybe I've had it with peas.

Looking forward to having your tea at mine as you know there will be peas? There won't be now. But, hey: tough peas!

The production slate of Brian May and Roger Taylor, Film Producers

Buoyed by the enormous global success of Oscar-winning biopic *Bohemian Rhapsody*, Queen stalwarts Brian May and Roger Taylor decided to take a well-earned break from playing the guitar on the roof of public buildings (and all those niggling attendant health and safety issues!) to bring more great stories to the silver screen/iPhone.

But some churlish people have questioned *Bohemian Rhapsody*'s verisimilitude: is this reality? Is this just an approximation thereof? Were Queen really playing that song on that particular tour (it doesn't matter)? Was Freddie's moustache quite right (who cares?)? And, of course, one particularly controversial issue ... In real life, Mercury was plagued by rumours that he might be an homosexual, something subtly alluded to in the film when Freddie mentions he quite likes disco.

Here we exclusively reveal the exciting projects that Brian and Roger have in development ...

Stonewall. A group of friends are relaxing in the sun-kissed garden of a Home Counties Harvester when the police arrive unexpectedly (don't they always?). The local special constable asks the friends if they are having a nice time, which they are.

Milk. Aptly named dairy farmer Harvey Milk enters the regional butter championships. Will his whey curdle in time?

The Naked Civil Servant. Happily married Department of Health and Social Care clerk Quentin Crisp gets on top of his filing.

Blue is the Warmest Colour. Interior decorator Adele Frenchlady just got serious! She's French. Long, bravura, authentic sequences of choosing colours from a colour chart exactly how interior decorators choose colours from a colour chart and not how other people like to get off on how interior decorators choose colours from a colour chart.

Brokeback Mountain. Two 1960s Wyoming sheep hands go about their business. Just to be clear, their business handling livestock.

Pride. A group of motivational speakers travel to south Wales to help local teenagers with their self-esteem. The minors reciprocate by coming to London to say thank you.

Oranges Are Not the Only Fruit. Greengrocer 'Big' Jim Winterson makes sure to offer a wide range of stock. 'Kiwis aren't the half of it. Even when it comes to citrus you've got to cover all the options these days,' he counsels. 'People will expect you to carry Easy Peelers.'

My Beautiful Laundrette. Working together to live the new '80s Thatcherite dream by charging people money to wash their clothes, Omar and Johnny briefly wonder if there might be more to their relationship. But of course there isn't! It all comes out in the wash. How they laugh.

Ask Greta

The Greta Thunberg-inspired climate actions pushed the environment to the top of the agenda, where it belongs. But the media – both mainstream and social – just had to canonise her, turning her into some sort of medieval icon, and become obsessed with her in ways that are slightly beyond comprehension.

Within a couple of weeks, they were asking her how to deal with Brexit. Give her a break: she's 16!

Here are some other genuine questions genuinely asked of the Swedish school student . . .

'Greta. Does God exist?'

'Greta. Who invented punk?'

'Greta. Why do the Americans pronounce aluminium the way they do? It's wrong and it's really annoying.'

'Greta. Which country is home to the most camels?'

'Greta. What is time? Is time travel possible, at least in theory?'

'Greta. If $\frac{1}{2}x + \frac{1}{2}(\frac{1}{2}x + \frac{1}{2}(\frac{1}{2}x + \frac{1}{2}(\frac{1}{2}x + \ldots) = y$, then $x = ?$'

'Greta. In terms of diseases that affect the elderly, how much of their origin is biological and how much can be ascribed to social reasons? And what do we do about it?'

'Greta. I have a two-part question. First, what is Beauty? And, also, second, what is Truth?'

'Greta. Edison or Tesla?' 'I don't understand the question.' 'You heard.'

'Greta. Can blind people see in their dreams?'

By the way, Malala does ads for Apple now. FACT!

I mean, she does other stuff, too. Obviously. But she does do that.

Donald Trump: The Literature

So it looks as though the presidency of Donald Trump will end up inspiring more books than that of almost any other President, many of whom could actually read books. *Should* Trump inspire books? Rather than, say, bumper stickers?

All these Trump works do make sense, though, if you consider that Donald Trump is essentially a fictional creation. Yes, he is technically non-fiction but he was certainly predicted by fiction: Orwell's *1984*, Sinclair Lewis's *It Couldn't Happen Here, The Simpsons.* All these and more predicted Trump's rise. Okay, only

The Simpsons actually predicted that Donald Trump would be elected President – to be honest, Orwell was way out on the specifics there. But anyway, as the stories attest, Trump had to happen. A hulking embodiment of Dumba$$ AmeriKKKa, a bragging, burger-munching cartoon imbecile elbowing his way to the top job having honed his playground-bully routine on reality TV: that was never not going to happen. Did you honestly think you'd get through your life without America electing Trump? You *knew* this was coming. Nothing is inevitable, of course it isn't – but this was.

Many varied works by wildly different creators are now available from all good bookstores, each one examining similar scenes from different perspectives – a bit like the Gospels, although we perhaps shouldn't get too carried away with the parallels to Jesus. Trump has already started to resemble one of those legendary characters endlessly reinterpreted through the ages – a little like Robin Hood, although we shouldn't get too carried away with the parallels to Robin Hood. For this reason, I have now read every single book about Donald Trump, from beginning to end, without skimming the boring bits, or the footnotes, and shall now dispense the wisdom gleaned about Donald Trump through the lens of the literature on Donald Trump, which he himself will not read, even though his name features all the way through.

Some of the books about Donald Trump that Donald

Trump will not read are the books that Donald Trump wrote. Except he didn't write them because Donald Trump can't write. But he can pay other people to write books by 'Donald Trump'. In 2011, Trump 'wrote' (didn't write) an, ahem, erotically charged blockbuster called *Trump Tower*, concerning all the dirty, dirty things people would do for a condo in the gold-plated skyscraper. The cover features the titular construction thrusting darkly into the sky; you could read this as a symbol akin to the *2001* monolith, an inscrutable pillar evoking everything and nothing: man's evolution, humanity's quest for a higher power, the eternal mysteries. I suggest that you do read it like this – the alternatives are not great.

But the most famous book (not) by Donald Trump is still 'his' 1980s bestseller *The Art of the Deal*, which dispenses key tips on how to succeed in real estate. He pours scorn, for instance, on the whole concept of 'location, location, location': 'You don't necessarily need the best location, you just need the best deal.' Don't worry, he doesn't pour scorn on *Location, Location, Location*. He's not a monster.

Has ghost-writer Tony Schwarz any regrets? Yes, he's had quite a few, actually: he now feels horribly culpable for birthing the central Trump mythos and has called him 'terrifying', a 'scared child' who is 'frightened by black people' and who lacks any abiding values or genuine feelings for another living soul. And he should know: he *is* Trump. Or was.

Couldn't he have expressed these concerns through the text, though, by way of warning? I don't necessarily expect: 'By the way, guys, he's – I mean, *I'm* – a terrified racist who can't even love my own children.' But maybe some hint somewhere? So if you read carefully between the lines, you might infer that the narrator character was a terrified racist who can't even love his own children. But frankly, who's got time for that?

Then there are the insider accounts of the Trump White House which, viewed together, convey a new hell where the only possible emotion is hate: everyone hates the President, the President hates everyone else and everyone else hates each other and themselves. You know the expression 'there's a lot of love in the room'? Well, there isn't in those rooms.

For the sake of brevity, let us distil some of these tell-all works to one key insult. Cliff Sims: 'vipers'. James Comey: 'chronic liar'. Bob Woodward: 'nervous breakdown of executive power'. Chris Christie: 'selfish'. (Subtle but damning, that last one.)

In her book *Unhinged*, former aide Omarosa Manigault Newman claimed that Trump privately wondered to her if he might be sworn in, not on the traditional Bible, but on 'the greatest business book of all time': *The Art of the Deal*. She advised him to not mention this idea to anyone else. 'We laughed. He wanted me to believe he was kidding.'

He wasn't kidding.

If nothing else, though, swearing on this one book that meant something to him would at least have been honest. And it does show a level of regard for the printed word that I for one find surprising. In the context of everything that has happened both before and since, would not the sight of Trump swearing an oath on *The Art of the Deal* by Donald Trump at least have been one gesture worthy of respect? No? Even in the *loosest* sense of the word? No?

Anyway, most famous of all is *Fire and Fury* by Michael Wolff, a journalist who gave the year-long impression of being a White House sofa cushion. They actually let him just sit and watch them for a year, taking notes. 'Don't mind me, I'm a sofa cushion,' he basically said, for a year, to the morons.

Among the many juicy takeaways from his account, I personally favour the revelation that national security adviser H. R. McMaster was fired for talking monotonously. 'That guy bores the shit out of me,' Trump declared, damningly.

Shouldn't someone have pointed out that McMaster's security briefings were not strictly speaking meant to be viewed as entertainment? I'm not suggesting they should have been *intentionally* boring, but, even if they were, this should not in and of itself have been a problem. You do have to wonder whether the President was going into these security briefings with the right set of expectations.

Then there are the cases for the defence. Given that there is no defence of Trump that possibly works in the realm of linguistic communication as understood and used by rational humans, you sometimes have to wonder what these writers are trying to achieve – although in the case of convicted fraudster Conrad Black, jailed for siphoning cash from his media empire, you don't have to wonder for long: on the publication of his lickspittle tome *Donald J. Trump: A President Like No Other* (he means it in a good way), he quickly achieved a Presidential pardon.

Then there is *Understanding Trump* by Newt Gingrich, architect of the Clinton-era fightback against liberal values in favour of bigotry and hate (not his words) (he called it 'the war'), which compares Trump to acknowledged national heroes like Abraham Lincoln and General George Marshall – flattering, but it does also genuinely feel like he's taking the piss. I like to think that this is the first in a series of Newt Gingrich *Understanding …* books and that he is currently working on *Newt Gingrich Understanding Love.*

Then there is Fox News presenter and one-time district attorney Judge Jeanine Pirro's offering, *Liars, Leakers and Liberals*, the alliterative title cunningly conveying the idea of a liberal wetting themselves and then blaming someone else – like they do! They totally do! In March 2019, Fox News was forced to suspend Pirro's show after she made Islamophobic comments on air. If Fox News thinks you've gone too far, then it's really very likely that you've gone too far.

In this work, she castigates the 'deep state' conspiracy against Trump and paints him as an all-round nice guy who doesn't hate immigrants at all. 'Does Donald Trump hate immigrants? No. Absolutely not.' Her crowning piece of evidence? 'The Trump Tower employees I spoke with who have foreign accents talked about what a great employer he is.' Case closed! Nice one, Judge!

I wouldn't recommend this as your first book in case it puts you off reading all other books. But it does raise important questions, like: where exactly the hell *is* this deep state when you need it? Hello, anti-democratic forces of the night, anyone home?!? Not that I'm into that kind of thing normally, but maybe just this once pull some shadowy cabal shit and just *get him out of there*?

I'm now actually starting to wonder: what if there *is* a deep state, and it's just quite shit at getting stuff done?

Then there are the Trump religious texts bearing titles like *The Faith of Donald J. Trump: A Spiritual Biography,* called 'a very interesting read' by none other than Donald Trump, who was presumably fascinated to find out about his spiritual beliefs (when it was read out to him). The link between Trump and evangelical Christianity sure is a strange one, what with him being the living embodiment of *all sins ever.* It turns out that some Christians are quite bad people. I *know*! It makes no sense! But as Jesus himself shruggingly declared: if thou canst not beat them, thou shouldst join them.

To be fair, the authors do tussle with the notion of this 'billionaire playboy' having any moral dimension, but they reason that, during all his 'pleasure-seeking' exploits, 'Trump has not lived apart from religion. In this regard, he is very American.' In his stinking hypocrisy, he's sort of an all-American hero! I guess there is a certain argument to be made: if Jesus died for all our sins, how much must he have died for Trump's sins? Jesus is probably *still* dying, out there somewhere, for Trump's sins.

Then there is *The Trump Prophecies* by 'prophet' Mark Taylor, a retired Florida firefighter who was told by God in 2011 that Trump would become President. And you thought he was just Chosen by the Russians and shadowy right-wing data miners. This raises another unsettling question: if God did indeed choose Trump to be President, what kind of god *is* God?

This tale was even adapted into a film by the right-wing evangelical Liberty University, founded by the ultra-conservative Reverend Jerry Falwell, a move which actually prompted protests from students who said, essentially, hold up there, that's too weird. If students at the right-wing evangelical Liberty University think you've gone too far, then it's really very likely that you've gone too far.

Some books simply stand alone, like *The Case for*

Trump by historian Victor Davis Hanson, who has divined that Trump fits into the mould of a classic tragic hero, 'a crude, would-be saviour who scares even those who would invite him in to solve intractable problems that their own elite leadership could not'. Quite seriously, Davis Hanson compares Trump to Achilles in Homer's *Iliad* and Ajax in Sophocles', er, *Ajax*. 'Unlike the duplicitous and smooth-talking Odysseus,' he notes, 'old Ajax lacks the tact and fluidity to succeed in a new world of nuanced civic rules.'

In essence, he might struggle to string words together but he does get the job done. The job in this case being 'tax cuts for the rich'. It's a powerful, cathartic tale. At the end, everyone dies.

For some reason, Hanson shies away from comparing Trump to Sophocles' most famous tragic hero: Oedipus. But given the President's reported relationship with his mother, this might have proved fruitful territory. 'Part of the problem I've had with women has been in having to compare them to my incredible mother, Mary Trump,' Trump wrote (didn't write) in another book, 1997's *The Art of the Comeback*.

So that's weird. But then come other reports that Trump in fact grew up 'very detached' from his mother, with some suggesting that this difficult, brittle relationship helps explain his whole motivation. 'What kind of son have I created?' she once reportedly asked his first wife Ivana, like Lee Remick in *The Omen*.

This abiding difficulty with female attachment perhaps sheds new light on his famous quote: 'Lock her up!' Lock *who* up, Donald? Which 'her' exactly are you talking about here? Didn't 'Hillary' love you enough? Did cool, brittle 'Hillary' create a little monster who forever lacked love and had to pepper the sky with more and more dark looming towers in a fruitless attempt to fill the unfillable void? Do you want to lock them *all* up, Donald? Is that what you're building all those towers for: so you can lock up all the women at the top of them? Is *that* what you were trying to tell us in *Trump Tower*? Grab them by the pussy? Grab them by the pussy indeed.

Sorry, got a bit dark there – but then I have been reading all the books about Donald Trump. And Donald Trump *is* a bit dark. Not clever-dark, like Moriarty or Magneto: stupid-dark. Like if Marlow had ventured up the river to find Kurtz was a money-grabbing moron with a fear of stairs: 'I'm telling you – the biggest horror! Just the biggest horror of all time!'

Finally, a little confession: I haven't even started *The Rabbis, Donald Trump, and the Top-Secret Plan to Build the Third Temple*. I always meant to, but you know what it's like.

It's up there now, on the shelf, staring out at me. Maybe one day!

The expanding Marvel Universe

With *Avengers: Endgame,* Marvel finally killed off a few (well, two) of its long-running superheroes. They will live on only in our memories, and in an endless succession of prequels and TV spin-offs. Here's a sneak preview of the whole new raft of great comic-book characters about to replenish the Marvel Universe . . .

Go Girl – More female empowerment.

Treason – A real antidote to all those patriotic superheroes. He's working *against* his own country!

Termite Man – Very, very similar to Ant Man.

Windrush – Landed in London from Jamaica in the years following the end of the Second World War.

The Assuager – Doesn't stop super-villains, but does help lessen their ill effects. Every time!

Gelatine – Contains animal products.

Mambo – Mama likes mambo, papa likes mambo. Look at 'em sway with it, shoutin' *Olé* with it!

TripAdvisor – Often comes in handy.

The Comestibles – Edible, but you've got to catch them first!

Spoiler – You always seem to know what he's going to do, because it was online.

Lavender – Smells nice.

Bulk – Often visits the cash and carry to stock up on non-perishables. Sometimes teams up with The Comestibles.

Whisper – Secretive and mysterious. But also quite hard to hear.

The Pedestrians – Watch out for the pedestrians.

The Cyclists – Watch out for the cyclists.

The Motorists – Watch out for the motorists.

The Electric Vehicles – Watch out for the electric vehicles (and beware: they make no noise!).

Deliveroo

Captain Czechoslovakia – steadfastly refusing to move with the times.

The Ladies of the Orient – Possibly problematic, for various reasons.

Uber-Eats – Deliveroo's nemesis.

Whatsit – cousin of The Thing.

Wotsit – an orange, cheesy, corn-based snack.

Dr Johnson

Assange

The Fart – Don't sit next to The Fart!

Will This Do? – a shitty minor-X-Man-level character that no one's really that into.

How many fucking platforms am I supposed to have to pay for just to watch the fucking telly?

Streaming. Everyone's at it. And why not? DVDs take up a lot of space. VHS cassettes? Massive. Having to wiggle the aerial? No thanks.

But, er . . . I really just want to watch the telly, and they won't let me. Well, they will, but I can only watch all this alleged abundance of great new content if I pay for 978 different streaming services. And fuck that for a game of soldiers. Or Thrones.

The old-school terrestrial channels can be confusing enough. *Love Island. Question Time. Posh Pawn.* There are a lot of programmes on. *Gogglebox*: that's lots of programmes on *all at the same time.*

People from *Gogglebox* doing ads in the ad breaks during *Gogglebox*: this is a level of complication we just do not need in our lives. I am trying to watch people watching telly. Now here they are, in the ad breaks, still watching telly, with me still watching them *on* the telly, but now they are trying to sell me something. It is *of Gogglebox* but is not *Gogglebox*. I'm not equipped for this.

Anyway, where was I? Ah yes . . .

Music? One platform will give you access to pretty much all the music that has ever been recorded. Most people will just listen to the platform's route one suggestions, but that's up to them. And the platform will only give the artist, who has rent their oeuvre from the deepest depths of their aching, broken soul, one three-thousandth of a thousandth of a thousandth of a halfpenny per stream. But that could be easily solved by them just giving the artists more money. It's so simple I'm surprised no one's thought of it before.

Telly? 978. You need 978 platforms. And, yes, I did count. There's Netflix of course, and Amazon Prime, and 976 other ones. Curzon, BFI, Sky . . . There's all sorts out there. Turns out *Homeland* was still on! Who knew?

Can I now trust that they are not trying to sell me something the rest of the time? The Malones always have cakes out. Are they subliminally advertising Sara Lee? Or Mr Kipling? Are they trying to make me buy a dog? I do not want a dog. I'd have to walk it and it would piss everywhere. What? Oh yes, streaming. I am not obsessed with this *Gogglebox* ads imbroglio. I'm just not.

And still more platforms are erected. Disney is taking a rare break from making too many Star Wars films – Q: How many Star Wars films are too many Star Wars films? A: The amount of Star Wars films that you are making – to launch TV platform Disney+. Why is it +? What the fuck does it mean? Disney+, AppleTV+ . . . Plus what? Surely it's just TV via Apple, amply described by the moniker AppleTV. Does it do chores for you or something? Is it code for 'contains adult channels'?

Anyway, one of the first major shows announced by Disney+ was, somewhat unpredictably, a Star Wars spin-off. Tremendous.

The BBC and ITV, not wanting to be left out, got involved with bollocks-named streaming service BritBox. BBC and ITV? I'm pretty sure I already have those. Anyway, as long as they keep ITV4 on the go they can knock themselves out. Do not axe re-runs of *Pie in the Sky*, *Lovejoy* or *The Professionals*. Don't take my ITV4 away – it's all I've got! And all those BBC4 documentaries I'm always pretending I've watched. The Vietnam War? Terrible business. Was Magna Carta really the start of English democracy? I just think there's more to it ... (I don't – I know fuck all about it!) ...

Gogglebox is on Channel 4 of course. Hence the ads. If the BBC bought it there would be no adverts, which would really help me out here. What are the couple in the Wiltshire cottage selling? Nature?

Steph and Dom may be gone, but they were filmed in their swanky B&B. Was that an ad? The Brighton hairdressers are obviously hairdressers. Would I want my hair cut by someone off *Gogglebox*? I just don't know! Leave me alone!

Almost one in five people (18 per cent) have admitted calling in sick to work to keep binge-watching a show. We watch for up to eight hours at a stretch. We go without sleep. Which makes us tired.

And almost a quarter of people (23 per cent) admit to having claimed to have watched something they haven't, so they don't get excluded by their peers. Is that right? For it to be socially unacceptable not to be on top of *Stranger Things*? 'I have a confession to make. I never did see the last season of *Breaking Bad*.' 'We aren't friends any more.'

Friends? That's still on. And apparently for a while was the biggest show in the world. Again. Maybe like every band that has ever existed now has to re-form and tour (it's on the statute book), they're trying to make every show ever made all be on all the time all at the same time. You know, just to see what happens.

Music of the Spheres? The Singularity? The Rapture? Or the Apocalypse? The only exception to the everything must be re-run rule is *It Ain't Half Hot, Mum*. For reasons unknown, *It Ain't Half Hot, Mum* never seems to get a re-run.

By the way, the *Radio Times*. Still exists! Do you think they have *all* the channels in it? And *all* the platforms? Maybe there are pensioners out there who have to spend half their pension on a minibus to get their gargantuan *Radio Times* home from Morrisons every week?

Or is it like it used to be (millennial readers might want to check their phones for this bit) (like you weren't already) and the *Radio Times* only has the BBC stuff in – so you also have to get *TV Times*, which is now the size of a shire horse?

Do you remember people asking if you remember Spangles?

Nick Clegg, Head of Global Affairs for the Apocalypse, responds to criticisms of the Apocalypse

The Apocalypse is under way. Over at the Radio 4 *Today* programme studio, Nick Clegg is talking to Justin Webb . . .

JUSTIN WEBB: Nick Clegg. The Apocalypse, for which you are the official spokesperson. Pestilence, war, plague, fantastic beasts ... it doesn't look good, does it?

NICK CLEGG: Look, with any difficult undertaking there will always be some naysayers who will focus on the wailing and the gnashing of teeth. But it's not all wailing and the gnashing of teeth. You've got to keep your eyes on the big picture here. Don't rush to judgement about the Judgement. That's what I've learnt. Look, I've had discussions with them and I like to believe that the Four Horsemen are, at the end of the day, reasonable people.

JUSTIN WEBB: Or at the end of days, even?

NICK CLEGG: Well, let's not get ahead of ourselves. The days have clearly not ended yet, Justin. So let's not get carried away by a few floods or random locust plagues.

JUSTIN WEBB: What's in this for you, Nick?

NICK CLEGG: It's not about me, Justin. You know that. And I know some people who will say, oh it's Nick Clegg – austerity and Facebook and all of that. I'm used to that. I've been in this game a long time now, Justin, and I have a massive house in California. Like, massive.

JUSTIN WEBB: And a place in the Afterlife?

NICK CLEGG: That's not for me to say, Justin. I won't be drawn on that. Look, people have been worried about climate change. And rightly so in my opinion. In a sense, this just brings the issue to the boil.

JUSTIN WEBB: An unfortunate metaphor, some might say. What about tuition fees?

NICK CLEGG: There are no tuition fees in Hell, Justin.

JUSTIN WEBB: Is that a cast-iron guarantee?

NICK CLEGG: Well, hang on there ... Look. It's about delivery. Delivering the Apocalypse. But delivering the fairest, most considered, most liberal Apocalypse we can. And I think that, if we can do that, then the end of the world need not be the end of the world.

JUSTIN WEBB: Nick Clegg, thank you.

NICK CLEGG: Thank you, Justin. By the way, you're on fire there a little bit ...

The craft beer revolution. Is it actually a revolution? Or more of a coup?

Most people who like beer – so-called beer drinkers, drinkers of beer – would probably agree that nice beer is nicer, nicer by far, than beer that is just all right or even, crivens, not nice.

But there's a slippery slope here, one that leads to purchasing a teeny-tiny tin of artisanal porter in a pub for £7.50.

How do they get away with charging £7.50 for a teeny-tiny tin of artisanal porter in a pub? It's not even draught! Surely the main point of pubs is to keep a range of fresh beer. If it's all bottles and tins, are they not then just a very expensive convenience store with seating (but no slightly past-it onions or scratchcards)?

I know these tins aren't just raw tin-coloured tins – they do have pictures of skulls on them and suchlike. But I can draw my *own* skull pictures for free. They won't be very good, but I don't care that much – I don't really *want* pictures of skulls.

And did I mention how small they are? They really are among the tiniest of all tins.

There are – fair's fair – many ways that the craft beer pioneers have added value to the whole pub experience. Changing the name to 'tap room', for example. Painting some of the wood black. Having functioning, non-wobbly stools (I do quite like the not-wobbling-around aspect of things).

But the main reason they can do this is *because people demand that they do.* Because, clearly, something can only be good if it is pricey. 'Yeah, I like this IPA [you would, mate, they all taste quite similar], but do you have a more expensive one?

'And maybe, you know, a bit *smaller*?'

Robert De Niro/Harvey Keitel ads for Brits: an review

People have called Robert De Niro a massive sellout for doing adverts for Warburton's. But what people don't realise is that he means this. *This* is his passion. A notoriously taciturn interviewee, get him on the subject of baked goods and he's suddenly Mr Won't Shut Up. Are you talking to him? About crumpets . . . ? You should do, because he loves them.

De Niro famously gained 60 pounds to portray the boxer Jake LaMotta's post-career decline in *Raging Bull*. How did he put on so much weight so quickly? Surely you know this: it was actually muffins and breadsticks and wraps. In the famous scene when he's knocked out in the ring, was it a mouthguard that went flying across the screen? Or a stray piece of bagel?

And remember De Niro as Jimmy in *Goodfellas*? We meet the wiseguy legend cruising around the hoods' bar/casino hangout handing out his trademark hundred-dollar tips to all and sundry. If De Niro had got his way, he wouldn't have been handing out hundred-dollar bills. His choice? Hundred-dollar Dunkin' Donuts gift cards.

'Marty, I just feel the character would be a bread man.'

'Bobby, how about a break. Sandwich? I got you pastrami on rye.'

'Light on the mayo?'

'Light on the mayo, Bobby – just like you like it. Let's just get the hundred-dollar bills thing in the can, then we'll try it your way . . .'

Harvey Keitel loves insurance: his admiration for the actuarial arts knows no bounds. He made Jane Campion's life hell during *The Piano* with his constant enquiries about whether they were still covered if they put the piano on the beach.

It's not an accident! Why do you think that, in the first place, the character he plays in *Pulp Fiction* is a man you call when things go to shit to come and clear it all up for you? That was his idea! They just edited out the bits where he checks the small print of the policy and tries to wriggle out of it.

Clearly, the two should do a remake of Scorsese breakthrough *Mean Streets*, reprising their roles as contrasting Little Italy brothers – one a livewire bad boy, one a guilt-ridden Catholic – this time giving proper prominence to crumpets and competitively priced insurance.

'I'm gonna stick this flatbread right up your ass!'

'Father, I have sinned . . . some of the dents were there before the accident . . .'

That kind of thing.

Coming soon: an film trailer

A cacophony of pages of a cacophony of books turn over, as if in the wind, all of a blur. *Sense and Sensibility, The Fellowship of the Ring, The Tale of the Flopsy Bunnies . . .*

Gravelly-voiced Voiceover Artist: 'In a world where there are lots of films being made about authors writing classic books, one author has obsessed the film-makers more than any other ... More than Jane Austen, more than J. M. Barrie, more than Tolkien or Beatrix Potter ... there was a man ... one man ... the man who brought you ... Winnie the Pooh ...

'First, there was *Christopher Robin ...*'

We see a sad-faced Christopher Robin (Ewan McGregor) entering a study where Evelyn Robin (Hayley Atwell) is doing architect stuff with architect gadgets at an architect's drawing table. 'Hello, Christopher Robin,' she says.

'Then there was ... *Goodbye, Christopher Robin*.'

A sad-faced Daphne de Sélincourt aka Mrs Milne (Margot Robbie) watches as her son Christopher Robin (Alex Lawther) exits the front door in his army uniform, heading off to war.

'Goodbye, Christopher Robin,' she says.

'And now ... Tom Hardy ... is ... A.A. Milne ... in ...'

Cut to Hardy as Milne in the Hundred Acre Wood, Sussex, England, with his top off, wielding a massive axe, blood plastering his forehead, next to a towering silver birch in a dappled glade. At the base of the tree is a yellow cartoon bear scooping honey from a pot, licking it from his paw.

'*... Winnie the Fucking Pooh*.'

We cut to Milne at his writing desk, doodling on a piece of paper. There is a drawing of a First World War tank with a German with a spiky helmet trying to get in through the hatch, crossed out; a drawing of a space adventurer fighting a large alien, crossed out; and a picture of a yellow cartoon bear . . .

Milne smiles and puts a tick next to the bear. 'Yes! I must to London.'

VO: 'There were good times . . .'

As Piglet (a piglet) looks on, Milne and Winnie the Fucking Pooh drop sticks off the side of a small wooden bridge over a narrow river, then run to the other side of the bridge to watch them pass through on the current.

Milne: 'Yes! Yes! I win! Fuck you! Yes!'

Milne, eyes gleaming, smears honey from a large pot all over his own face. Then he starts having flashbacks to some sort of occult ceremony from his past.

VO: 'There was friendship . . .'

Milne and Eeyore, a cartoon donkey, are in the snug bar at the Anchor Inn in Hartfield, Sussex, taking slugs of whisky. They have been drinking heavily all afternoon.

Milne: 'You're a goddam miserable bastard, Eeyore – but we are one.'

Eeyore falls off his stool. Milne throws his head back and roars with laughter – and then, as he catches a glimpse of the landlord, falls immediately, suddenly silent.

Milne: 'You. Fight me if you do not afear me!'

Cut to Milne, his head now shaved, charcoal markings on his cheeks, climbing a tree high up in the Ashdown Forest.

As he reaches the top, Milne looks out over the forest canopy and bellows: 'Hon-eeeeeey!'

VO: '*Winnie the Fucking Pooh*. Coming Soon.'

A caption appears, words slamming onto the screen one at a time, accompanied by a thud:

WINNIE

THE

FUCKING

POOH.

Fade to black. The black in our hearts.

Brexit means Brexit? A Brexit glossary

Have you been confused by Brexit? You say you haven't, but actually you have. And that's okay. Here is the definitive A–Z of the whole shebang.

Article 50. Was triggered by hand-delivered letter. How quaint! Had they not heard of email? Or were they just anticipating the point where we wouldn't be allowed to email other countries? The letter was delivered by the traditional urchin child, paid in coal.

Berlin Time. The EU spent years quietly trying to assume the power to bend time. Well, to stop us changing our clocks twice a year, from GMT to BST (British Summer Time: best summer time in the world) and back. They claim that 'numerous scientific studies' (ha!) show no benefits to the clock changes. In fact, research (ha!) has suggested that, in the days after the clocks are changed, elderly people are more susceptible to heart problems, it messes with agriculture, road accidents go up and children's academic performance goes down. So what? We *like* changing our clocks. The EU has considered making us adhere to EU Summer Time, GMT plus two hours, or we could have GMT all year round. Or the one they really wanted us to adhere to was Central European Standard Time, an hour ahead of GMT; or, to give it its proper name, as designated by the *Express*, Berlin Time. Berlin Time? *Of course* they want to put us on Berlin Time. Always have, always will. Do not change our clocks, Europe. We have always changed, and will always change, our own clocks.

Bollocks. Swearing: not big (it is), not clever (it is). At their campaign launch for the 2019 European elections, the Liberal Democrats revealed their main campaign slogan: BOLLOCKS TO BREXIT. 'We are credible,' said then-leader Vince Cable, standing next to the word BOLLOCKS. And it said BOLLOCKS next to him because he had put it there. BOLLOCKS BOLLOCKS BOLLOCKS – that's them. They are *all about* BOLLOCKS. Asked if the Lib Dems were coarsening public discourse, Vince Cable replied: 'Go fucking fuck yourself, you massive prick.'

Brexit comprehension lag. The Irish did their first study into the effects of a pro-Brexit vote in 2014, while Britain was still thinking that you might just as well plan for The Rise of the Krakens, led by Godot. Perhaps

Ireland was the nation best placed to know how weird Britain can sometimes get? Britain spent 2014 mostly thinking about the Apple Watch, David Moyes and Caroline Flack winning *Strictly*.

Brexit hampers. In January 2018, a delegation of Brexiteers – Steven Woolfe MEP, Lord Digby Jones (yep, he's still here), John Mills (the Labour donor, not the late actor) and chair of the Leave Means Leave campaign John Longworth – presented EU chief negotiator Michel Barnier with a hamper of classic British products in Brussels. The hamper contained great British items such as Marmite, Piccalilli, Cheddar cheese, a biography of Winston Churchill and gin, and was designed to introduce Barnier to staples from this exotic land. 'Weee,' said Jones very, very slowly, 'Weee – co-me – ac-ross – [does a wavy hand] the – sea. Weee bri-ng cheeeese. Youu like cheeese. Youu for-eign. Weee [indicates his fellows] British. Bri-tish . . .' 'Thank you,' responded Barnier, and the Brexiteer delegation jumped out of their skins as if they had seen a horse talk.

The Brexit March. It began, like all the best British outdoor adventures, in a car park in the rain. In March 2019, Nigel Farage led his people across the soggy fields of County Durham. Just like Moses. Then he left them to it. Again, like Moses. They were marching on the capital to Take Back Control. Did they even get there in the end? Seriously, I don't actually know. Does anyone know? Are they still walking now?

'Brexit means Brexit.' On one level, of course it does. Brexit means Brexit. Leave means Leave. No means no. But what *does* it mean? Seriously: what? This slogan for a Theresa May speech was presumably invented to signify no-nonsense sturdiness. But then she started using it in negotiations, with negotiators, when they asked her what Brexit *really* meant. Repeatedly. It was important to them, they felt, that they understand what Brexit meant, because they were trying to negotiate Brexit. They really wanted to know! But it was a secret.

Brexit Party. A retired railway worker at a Brexit Party rally in Nottingham explained the appeal: 'Nelson, Winston Churchill, Margaret Thatcher, Ian Botham and Nigel Farage – they're the people who put the Great into Britain.' Well, on a strictly factual level Nelson was definitely part of building the so-called British Project, aka world domination, aka the Empire. Winston Churchill tried to maintain, but ultimately lost, the Empire. Margaret Thatcher cheerfully sold off the country to foreigners. Ian Botham famously played cricket for England, and England is not the same as Britain, believe it or not. And Nigel Farage is just a prick.

Celebrity Leavers. Michael Caine, Theo Paphitis, Frederick Forsyth, the late Keith Chegwin, James Dyson, Sol Campbell, Bernie Ecclestone, Sam Allardyce, Tariq Ali, Joan Collins, John Cleese ... 'Bring it on you ranting luvvies, fat cat bankers and multinational corporations. Continue to alienate the humble voice of Middle

England. Knock yourselves out calling us ill-educated Neanderthals and spit a bit more venom and vitriol our way. You are showing yourselves in all your mean-spirited, round-headed, elitist glory,' said, er, Liz Hurley, sticking it to the round-headed elites once again. 'Run to the hills,' said Iron Maiden frontman Bruce Dickinson, 'Run for your life.' Not about the EU, but also, yes, about the EU.

Children's creativity. Brexit has inspired the children, the wonderful children, the children. A survey – conducted by lexicographers at the Oxford University Press – of the 100,000-plus entries to the 2019 Radio 2 short story competition crowned 'Brexit' the 'children's word of the year'. The words 'backstop' and 'no deal' (and this is true) also featured heavily in a myriad of stories about trying to do a Brexit deal, help the beleaguered Mrs May or just cancel Brexit (isn't *The Beleaguered Mrs May* a David Walliams book?). The kids' titles included 'The Cat Who Solved Brexit' and 'A Unicorn Called Brexit'. And we all lived happily ever after. Ha!

Chlorinated chicken. Then-International Trade Secretary Liam Fox said that leaving the EU would allow the UK to free itself of nonsense red tape like food standards and start importing cheap-as-chips chlorinated chicken from the US. Chlorinated chicken. Chicken so foul (sorry) that it has had to be cleaned with chlorine. Is that good? It doesn't sound good, given that chlorine is used to sterilise swimming pools chock-full of verruca flakes and child urine (and some adult urine: you know who you are). Fox said 'the British public' should have the 'choice' to eat chlorinated chicken. Although presumably one can assume he wouldn't 'choose' to serve it at his own soirées?

Confirmation bias. According to polls, the allegedly more cosmopolitan Remainers were less likely to know Leavers than vice versa. So there must be a few promiscuous Remainers who are getting to know all kinds of Leavers. Please note: this does not mean they are having sex with each other. Inter-tribal sex! Thrilling, possibly. But frowned upon.

Constructive ambiguity. Labour's approach to the big issue of the day: try not to come down firmly as either Leaver or Remainer. Increasingly came to look like kicking the can down the road. Challenged on this, the Labour leader said: 'What can?'

Continental quilts. The continent (*the* continent? There are other ones, you know!) is mostly famous for only two things: continental breakfasts and continental quilts. Continental breakfasts we can probably do without, cake and cheese not being the best of breakfasts. But you don't think the Brexiteers will ban duvets? You know, bring back sheets and blankets? That would be a real fag (*all that folding*, and the claustrophobia).

Yvette Cooper. Does not like Brexit. Not even one bit. Clearly going about things in the only way she knows how, and to a certain extent *c'est la vie* – but if you look up 'political class technocrat trying to stop Brexit via bureaucratic stitch-up' in the dictionary, you will see a picture of Yvette Cooper. And, okay, I put it there, but so what?

Deal or no deal. A long-running gameshow hosted by Noel Edmonds.

ERG. Worst WhatsApp group ever.

Ferries. When is a ferry not a ferry? When it isn't a ferry.

Foreign language GCSEs. The take-up of foreign language GCSEs has fallen dramatically, many parents seeing them as a waste of time because of Brexit. Quite right. Time to open the curriculum to include talking loudly and slowly, while pointing at what you want. Foreigners respect us more when we do that.

'Fuck "Fuck business"'. With the Lib Dems owning the word 'bollocks', the Tories started saying 'fuck' a lot. Boris Johnson famously said, 'fuck business'. Short-lived leadership hopeful Matt Hancock continued the debate, saying: 'Fuck "Fuck business".' At which point, I honestly assumed someone else would pipe up: 'Fuck "Fuck 'Fuck business'".' With someone else then saying – well, you get the picture. Come on Tories, get your fucking saying fuck shit together!

Uri Geller. Defeating Brexit via mind control. Did he make the pipes burst and flood the Commons in early April 2019, as he suggested? No, he did not. Or did he? No. Or did he? Friend of Michael Jackson, of course. That's just a literal observation, by the way, not a euphemistic coining to accuse people of being paedos. What was that flood anyway? A Biblical Flood – a punishment from God? Old plumbing? Or the institution itself enjoying a spot of situational irony?

Grand Wizards. Elite leaders of the Ku Klux Klan. Oh, and 'elite' leaders of the Brexiteers, who just *used the same name as* the KKK. So that's all right then.

Greek crisis. Worth remembering.

***Guardian* readers.** People who read the *Guardian* newspaper, either the print version or online.

Halloween extension, the. They never even did Halloween here till the noughties. Tell kids of today that and they won't believe you! Landlines, dial-up modems and a lot less chocolate. Desolate times. The choosing of this date for a Brexit extension was proof that at least someone in the negotiations has a sense of humour. Or is evil. Or both.

Having your unicorn and eating it negotiating strategies. Back in 2018, Boris Johnson showed his early-doors leadership skills by saying we could 'have our cake and eat it' – so speedily displaying to all concerned that they were dealing with people who lived in fucking Narnia. Then people started talking about unicorns. Basically, if we could square the Irish border circle, then we would find our unicorn, eating a cake, which remains a cake despite (or because of?) (think about that) being eaten? If you do ever come across a unicorn – a real one, not just a horse with a horn stuck to its head, I've been burned by that shit just *too many times* – then do *not* eat the unicorn.

No: exhibit the unicorn and charge people to see it. What are you, some sort of moron?

'I'll never vote again!' You will though, won't you?

Keir Starmer's hair. I think we can all mostly accept Jeremy Corbyn looking a shambles. It's his thing. But surely Keir Starmer, *Sir* Keir Starmer, barrister and would-be Brexit Secretary, should, before going on the telly or making a statement in the House, brush his fucking hair? Standards, man, standards! (On a similar tip, one concerned citizen had quite a pertinent question to put to London Mayor Sadiq Khan in a December 2018 Q&A for *Time Out*: 'Do you not own a tie?')

Managed Deal with access to *a* Customs Union but not *the* Customs Union with Cooper bolted on but not Boles then Cooper taken off again and merged with Malthouse, to be confirmed by a non-binding referendum which takes place only in Scotland . . . The *obvious* solution and what they should have done in the first place! Just get on with it! Whatever 'it' is.

Max fac. A brand of cosmetics.

Maximum facilitation. Magic, non-existent technology that would somehow (no one knew) check goods coming into the country. Mooted by Brexiteers who quite like the whole streamlined customs arrangement thing. That is, being in the EU. But don't like the EU. But don't not like the EU enough. Lightweights, basically. Come on, if you're not up for some proper border argy-bargy, with lorries parked up literally everywhere, the whole country stinking of piss, then your heart's not in it.

MPs you'd never heard of before. Brexit has revealed a seemingly endless stream of MPs ready to pop up on the news and give their twopenn'orth. What are they doing in there? Breeding them? Cloning them? Some have become household names and you find yourself asking, 'How have I ended up knowing quite so much about Lisa Nandy?' But always there are more. Pronouncing in the lobby or on the panel on *Peston*. Peston always seems to know who they are. How does he manage to retain all that information? Maybe it's why he wears his hair a bit long: bit of weight to keep all those MPs' names in his bonce.

The naked anti-Brexit protester. That is, Victoria Bateman, the Cambridge economist who went on the *Today* programme and then the telly, in the buff, in order to stop Brexit stone dead, by being in the buff. 'Brexit Leaves Us Naked,' she said, and also wrote on her body. The evidence was stark(ers): Brexit *was* happening and Victoria Bateman *was* naked. But had Brexit left Victoria naked or had she just taken all her clothes off? Whatever; her body, her choice, and it was all tastefully pixelated by Auntie. And anyway: how better to illustrate the view that Brexit would leave us naked than by actually being naked? Is this right, though? I mean, if I'd wanted to argue the point that a No Deal Brexit would be a bit like the country hitting itself in the face with a hammer, I'd definitely not go on the telly and hit myself in the face with a hammer. But maybe that's just me. Sadly, the idea that the sight of a naked lady might sway certain stereotypical Brexit voters was dealt a blow when a former editor of *Loaded* came out publicly for the Brexit Party. Leave or Remain? Kit on or kit off? Sadly, the nation remained divided.

NHS on the table. Of course the NHS was on the table, said Trump, referring to any new US trade deal. No it wasn't, said the Tories. And Trump agreed. The Brexiteers would rather die than let US private healthcare providers get their hands on 'our' NHS. Although, of course, the NHS has been 'on the table' – that is, steadily carved up by profiteers – for some years now. Hands off! Unless they're already on ... Shhh. Don't tell anyone.

No deal preparations. Only by preparing for 'no deal' will you get a deal, which you need, because you really don't want 'no deal'. But don't say you don't want 'no deal', because then you're where they want you, with 'the deal'. They will tell you that there is already a deal, and that it is a 'done deal', but there is another deal. You know there is. A better deal. For special occasions. Of course there is. There must be. Surely? By now, you will have even confused yourself about whether you want a deal or want a no deal. Only then will you be getting somewhere. And that is how to do a deal. Or a no deal. Or both. Or neither. Or both.

Ode to Joy. The Brexit Party's newly elected MEPs turned their backs on musicians playing this section from Beethoven's Ninth, the so-called 'anthem' of the EU, at the start of the new European Parliament. Some people seem to aspire to become a living metaphor: they turned their backs on European culture, by turning their backs on European culture. Ode to Joy? No to Joy! Meanwhile, the Lib Dems wore T-shirts with the word BOLLOCKS on them and Green Party MEP Magid Magid got into a bit of argy-bargy and ended up on the street outside. Quite a classically Brits Abroad day all round, really. They had a right old sing-song on the coach home.

The People. Basically, everyone who agrees with you. Should be listened to. To be contrasted with people who don't agree with you, who should go and fuck themselves.

People's Vote. Should happen, or has happened, depending on your point of view. (See: The People.)

Radio ads for the EU Resettlement Scheme. Soothing, soft, silky-voiced government ads reassuring EU citizens they will be welcome to stay after Brexit, as long as they fill in a teensy-weensy form. In stark contrast to the hostile environment and the time Theresa May sent vans round with the words 'JUST – FOR – FUCK'S – SAKE – FUCK – OFF – YOU – SPONGING – SHITS!' on them. (Still, for God's sake do not fill the form in: THAT'S HOW THEY GET YOU!)

Red Lines. A stupid idea. Also, the video was really sexist.

Remoaners. Is it possible to despise the people who use this term of abuse while also finding yourself hugely irritated by the people it's aimed at? Yes, it is possible. Is it okay? Yes, it is okay.

Remoaner tat. Tatty Devine 'European' necklaces, saying the word 'European' (in blue, with a yellow star attached) (25 quid), to express how 'European' you are, and also what a tool you are. You can also get blue T-shirts featuring the EU circle of stars with one star missing and the slogan in the middle: 'I am quite cross.' There are pro-EU can coolers, for people who hate Brexit like they hate warm cola: a lot!

You can get bumper stickers saying 'No Brexit', although you don't see many around. Remainers like talking about how awful Brexit is, but are less keen on their car getting keyed.

A word of complaint here: it is very difficult to spoof you if you are basically a spoof of yourself in the first place. (Note to self: finally get round to putting those 'Knit your own yogurt!' tea towels on Amazon. That Ardennes holiday home will not buy itself.)

Remoania. A mythical land where everyone sits outside cafés reading voguish foreign translation novels, talking about hot yoga and eating pastries (not pastry). The sun always shines in Remoania.

Singapore. We could be like Singapore! I like

Singapore Noodles, so maybe it would be good? Oh, no – they actually mean low business taxes and no rights. And it won't be as hot. And I can already get Singapore Noodles. They are quite widely available, I have found. Beware of investigating Singapore's appeal, though. Arch-Brexiter James Dyson so convinced himself that the UK and businesses like his would be better off leaving the EU and becoming more like Singapore that he ended up just cutting to the chase and moving both himself and his business to Singapore. Cheers for that.

Stockpiling. Bringing a new, less fun meaning to the phrase 'Get some tins in!'

Sunlit uplands. Sound good, are good. Not happening.

Taking back control. It's all about taking back control! In order to then give it to right-wing demagogues funded by shadowy billionaires who keep their money offshore.

Tariffs. In March 2019, the government announced what would happen to prices in the event of a No Deal Brexit. The price of cars would go up but underpants would go down (hur hur – underpants would go down. I said underpants would go down). Peas, for some reason, would go up. And I thought post-Brexit Britain was going to be *all about* driving around in my new motor in my new 'for best' pants, with a big bowl of peas. Time for a rethink. Again!

Tennyson. Victorian poet. Bor-or-ing. At a pro-Brexit

event, Tory MP and proper hardman Mark Francois read all 70 lines of Tennyson's 'Ulysses'. Was he comparing himself to the mythic hero of the title? That is for others to say. And you can quote selectively, you know – you don't have to read the whole thing.

***That* bus.** Look: who doesn't want loads of fish and an extra £350m a week? Makes a change from adverts for films that were out two years ago.

Treason, traitors, betrayal, surrender, appeasement, collaboration ... Just some of the entirely proportionate language that can be used in pubs, or national newspapers, to describe the abject failure to just get on with it. As veteran Europhobe Bill Cash, an MP, put it in the *Telegraph*, a newspaper: 'How low can we sink with the Prime Minister making us crawl on our hands and knees, not only to the EU, but to Germany and France?' Not just Italy, yeah, where he once had a nice holiday, or even Romania where his man got him a decent drop of red which was quite the bargain, but the fucking Nazis and the surrender monkeys! I'd go further: paedos, mate, the lot of them. Oh come on, it's not like you weren't thinking it.

'Unleashing demons of which ye know not'. Shakespeare? The Bible? No, David Cameron. It was in fact David Cameron waxing uncharacteristically lyrical on what calling a European referendum might do, just before he called a European referendum. 'Fuck it,' he added: 'Yolo!' He lives in a shed now.

WAB. Taking her shitty Brexit deal back to the

Commons for the fourth time, Theresa May tried the very cunning strategy of changing its name and then also turning that name into an acronym. It worked, but only for five minutes – when the canard was uncovered and the shitty deal voted down once more. Shitty Brexit deal *means* shitty Brexit deal, or SBD if you will.

'Where were the EU in the Falklands?' This question, tweeted in to LBC, might – might – be the greatest sentence ever written.

WTO rules. Not sure. Something to do with racing cars in America?

Is it okay to fuck up the Earth as we can just go and live on Mars?

No.

Who owns space?

I mean, someone must. It can't just be *there*, surely?

Maybe when humans finally land on another planet, an alien bailiff will pitch up and tell them to fuck off. Who can say?

In the late 1970s, the United Nations legislated for humanity to share space. The Moon, which the Americans had been pretending they had managed to visit for a full decade by this point, was declared off-limits for exploitation. The Moon was everyone's to share. A common treasury for all.

It's a beautiful vision. But, like so many things the United Nations gets up to – say, sending peacekeepers to Bosnia who then engage in a spot of light sex-trafficking – there's more to it. The only countries who incorporated the Moon Treaty into their own national law were ones that had no means of getting to space. They were cool with not doing something they couldn't do anyway. It's so often the way.

The countries that actually could monetise space were far less keen on not being allowed to monetise space. The Americans, in particular the Republicans, were having none of the not monetising and resisted all efforts to enshrine the Moon's new commonwealth status into US law. They were quite keen on bringing 'freedom' to extra-terrestrial bodies and taking away any cool resources: for oil, see metals, minerals, photon torpedoes . . .

What would the UN do anyway? Send observers? 'Yeah, we've looked into it and they are definitely fucking shit up up here . . . Like, big time . . .' Then the sex-trafficking would begin (presumably over on the Dark Side).

Back then, only nation states were in the space race. These days, you can get involved at home: companies with names like Planetary Resources and Deep Space

Industries are open to investors looking to make an extra-terrestrial buck. Silicon Valley billionaires are on board. Of course they are. And so is the government of Luxembourg. Well, they missed out on the scramble for colonies on Earth and don't want to get burned with that shit again. (Luxembourg was even a colony itself for a while, a colony of Spain. You can see why they're keen to get on top of this.)

Is space the ultimate investment opportunity? To all intents, it's infinite. The only drawback is that the space mining companies, which exist and you can invest in, don't have any way of getting to the minerals, or the technology to mine them if they did. So you'd be giving money to people to mine minerals they don't own, can't reach and don't know how to mine. It's a long-term investment.

So humans are up for mining space. Literally. A single asteroid could yield billions of dollars of material. If you could mine one. Which you can't. Thus far only four missions have landed anything at all on an asteroid, let alone consumed the asteroid and brought its bounty back home. The only thing that has been returned to the Earth from an asteroid was a very small amount of dust, by the Japanese in 2005. It wasn't even enough to constitute a handful, so wasn't even much use as a metaphor. And haven't we got plenty of dust down here already?

But we'll probably get there eventually. Mining equals hard cash. Mining also equals waste, spoliation and slag. Given access to other planets, will humans just fuck them up? The evidence isn't good. Of all the planets we've had access to so far, we've fucked up 100 per cent of them. Which is, if you think about it, an absolutely terrible failure rate – you literally couldn't get any worse at not fucking up planets. And, yes, that's a sample of only one single planet, which is a very small sample – you couldn't get any lower without going to no planets at all. But all the more reason not to fuck it up, if it's the only one you've got.

So unless we take some kind of evasive action, it'll be like the Wild West up there, in space, and that would not be good. Space cowboys sound fun, but they wouldn't be. Han Solo is an exception, because he's good deep down (you know that).

What we really need are some ground rules, preferably before we leave the ground – possibly the best time to decide something is bad and unacceptable being before it has already happened.

'Take care up there. You remember what happened the last time? That's right, you fucked it up . . .'

The Independent Group/Tiggers/Change UK/whatever they're called this week, presuming they still exist: death throes of crap centrism? Surely?

2019 and politics is broken. Really broken. Fucked, basically. We needed heroes. And heroes assembled.

Chuka Umunna, Heidi Allen, Anna Soubry, the other ones whose names no one can remember, not really, not if they're being honest ... But 11 good women and men so true. Coming to clean out the stables and wash the scum off the streets. Broken politics: Endgame.

And didn't it go well? From seven MPs resigning from the Labour Party and launching the Independent Group to Chuka Umunna doing one (again) and joining the Lib Dems took 115 days. Or less than four months. And was the face of British politics forever changed? Was it fuck.

Did they Icarus it, and fly too close to the sun? No, they were the collective Shit Icarus that didn't even fly but just plunged straight into the briny. 'Look at me, Da, I'm King of the ... Oh shit! Fuck! ... Aaaaarggghh!' – that kind of vibe.

What was the best bit? Was it, on launch day, the now-former Labour MP Angela Smith, who no one had ever heard of, taking time out of a hectic schedule to do a racism on live TV? She hadn't got the memo that no one says 'funny-tinged people' any more. The memo from 1978. Still: now they've heard of her!

Was it the fact the Tiggers had no policies? They simply could not stay in their respective parties. Yes, Brexit. Or rather, no, not Brexit. No thanks. But more. So much more. Their mission was nothing less than to forge a new politics. Forge it in their fire. What politics, they were asked. Eh, they said. What politics, they were asked again. Er, allsorts.

It was their destiny to found a new party of the centre. They could not just join the Liberal Democrats, the established centre party already obsessively opposed to Brexit, as it was an established party and thus by definition broken. Politics was broken. Politics? Broken. They had heard the people's siren call. Well, Chuka said he'd had some encouraging conversations with friends in the media, so there was that.

Soubry said she still supported austerity, while Chuka said he really didn't, all told. Allen said people should just leave them alone. They'd literally just split from their former parties as part of a burning mission to renew politics. They couldn't also be expected to say what their politics were. Not now. They'd announce policies, she said, 'after Christmas'. New Year, new policies!

Let's just get Christmas out of the way they said, in the spring. Well, some people do take Christmas very seriously. That five-bird roast won't stuff itself into itself into itself into itself!

Was the best bit them avowedly splitting from their parties to undertake the urgent work of uniting all the anti-Brexit forces and then, as soon as the Euro elections were announced, registering themselves as a political party just in time to refuse to unite with any other anti-Brexit forces and stand under their own banner?

Or them having some trouble designing said

banner? Or agreeing what they were called ... At their public launch for the elections, the TIGs had placards printed in a variety of *different individual colours* (red, purple, yellow, black ...), with *both* Change UK *and* The Independent Group written on them. They also randomly changed their Twitter handle from @indgroup to @forchange_now, only to see the original taken by an arch-Brexiter. (They later announced that, on the Euro election ballot papers, their party name would be listed as Change UK The Independent Group.) (Although they knew they'd have to dump that name after the election as the change.org website had threatened legal action.)

Gavin Esler, Rachel Johnson and the singer from 1990s band the Longpigs might have been announced as candidates, although that definitely sounds like the sort of thing that happens in dreams when you have the flu or have been drinking.

Was the highlight The Whatevers managing 3 per cent of the vote, with no TIG MEPs elected, while the 'broken' Lib Dems got 20 per cent?

Was it that the thing they clearly spent most time on – literally, like, a generation – was deciding where to chow down for a collective meal? After all, they wouldn't want to do a George Osborne – tweeting a picture of his burger to show he's One of Us, only to be derided because it was a swanky Byron burger. So, a 'cheeky' Nando's it was. Peri-peri populism.

Did they spend more time nailing down where to be

pictured eating than they did discussing policies? I'm not saying they did, even though they did, but they did. Why is Nando's 'cheeky' anyway?

Smith apparently ordered the lemon and herb chicken, the blandest thing on the menu. Perhaps she's not a fan of spicy food? Soubry ordered bottled water. Why not just stab a polar bear through the fucking throat?

Was it Umunna, who had previously written that he could 'never forgive' the Lib Dems for what they had done to his constituency, Streatham, by propping up the austerity coalition – and who was apparently the author of an internal TIG discussion document pledging to 'destroy' the Lib Dems (asset-stripping their donors, poaching their members, taking their votes ... crushing the fucking life out of them, basically) – joining the Lib Dems?

They made him Treasury Spokesperson. Of course they did. It's a dirty job but someone's got to do it.

Broken politics? Yeah: you fucking broke it.

Allen, the leader, left when Umunna did. As did another four of the MPs – so that's six MPs from a total of 11. Anna Soubry assumed the leadership (of course she did). Soubry said Umunna had 'made a very serious mistake' by leaving, which when written down sounds like a threat of violence. I'm pretty sure it wasn't, though. (Having said that, she was accused of running Change UK 'like a Soviet state'. Of course she was.)

They changed the name again – because, well,

they hadn't done that for a couple of weeks – to the Independent Group for Change. The Independent Group for Change had now finally had more names than colour schemes. And only one fewer than its tally of MPs.

The split from the split (minus the new Lib Dem Treasury Spokesperson) were now an independent group. Not *the* Independent Group. No: they were a group now independent of the Independent Group (that is, The Independent Group, or Change UK, or Change UK – The Independent Group, aka the Independent Group for Change). Were they still even for change? To be honest, I've lost track a bit.

The media-friendly centrists have been telling us to leave it to them for decades now. Nothing – not the financial crash, austerity, the failure to address the coming climate disaster – seems to puncture their self-satisfied belief in their own powers. Despite most onlookers thinking they wouldn't trust them to feed their cat while they were on holiday.

But surely this – the collective Shit Icarus – will finally puncture the (Westminster) bubble? From bullshit and riding a media buzz to crash, collapse, rejection, rats jumping ship and being run by a 'Soviet' advocate of austerity. In what? Less than two school terms?

Will they learn? Will they fuck. *Everything* changes. Except this lot.

Even after Umunna and Allen had done one and Shit

Icarus was bobbing about in the sea, taking on water, Soubry still clung to the dream – letting us know far too much about the fever dream that had also been something that had happened …

She confided: 'I will always be more sad than you can imagine that Chuka is not with us [bloody hell – he's not dead!]. I think he's a man of huge ability and talents …

'I believed in him, and believed he should be Prime Minister of our country.'

Prime Minister! Fucking hell! She would never have let austerity come between them. And, to be fair, Chuka didn't let it come between him and never never-forgiving the Lib Dems. Maybe nothing matters?

Still, they'll always have Nando's.

At the time of writing, Chuka Umunna is not the Prime Minister.

The robot/AI takeover: has it already happened?

If the robots *were* going to take over (they are), would they announce it first?

No, they would not. They're not stupid. They're *very* clever. It's sort of the point of them. But has Artificial Intelligence – or, to use its proper technical name, Skynet – already assumed power over the humans? Consider the evidence …

Manchester City: football robots

Manchester City players are clearly robots and manager Pep Guardiola is clearly their robot overlord. This much is obvious.

With their clinical demolition of opponents, Man City have turned watching a game of association football into a pursuit more akin to watching people play video games on YouTube. And, yes, many people enjoy watching people play video games on YouTube, but is it that satisfying, at the end of the day?

Man City's 6–0 FA Cup Final win over Watford rendered it one of the most soulless cup finals ever. It had the joint highest winning margin in cup history, but you have to go back to 1903 for the other one. Bury did also beat Derby 6–0, but only because, even in an age of voluminous shorts, Derby had shorts so big (pantaloons, really) that they kept getting blown about in the wind. And they were really pissed.

But Man City won 6–0 because – clearly – they are robots.

Tech experts are divided over whether the young Guardiola was replaced by a full automaton, or had robot technology gradually fused into his organic body. Proponents of the first theory point out that if you compare pictures of the young Pep Guardiola, hoofing a ball about in midfield for Barcelona, he doesn't actually look much like the Pep you see now, and that isn't all down to that weird cardie thing he wears (robot!). They definitely do not look the same. Supporters of the organic theory point to a gradual transformation as the technology was introduced: as they implanted more chips into his brain, they say, Pep gradually lost the ability to grow hair on his head. He hides this evident truth by having stubble on his chin which, this tech faction contends, is just 'stuck on'.

Like any good algorithm, Guardiola hungrily hoovers up information. When he pitched up as manager of Bayern Munich he could mysteriously already speak fluent German. Maybe he learned? Yeah: machine-learned. When he was preparing to start his career in management, he systematically went round to renowned managers and asked them their secrets. When he visited former Argentina manager Marcelo Bielsa, he questioned him for 11 hours straight. 'There are 36 different forms of communicating through a pass,' Bielsa has said (he wasn't just plucking numbers out of the air. He's got a list somewhere . . .). Guardiola took all this information, crunched it through his robot brain and calculated this conclusion: buy all the most expensive players in the whole world. If any of the purchases fail to bed in or don't pan out, just buy another one. More than one: fuck it, why not? Then turn them into robots.

But does it get worse? It does. It always does. Despite winning the Premier League, FA Cup and EFL Cup that season, Man City missed out on a place in the 2019 Champions League final when they lost the semi-final to Spurs. Despite the two-leg tie being a draw, 4–4, Spurs went through on away goals, Llorente having scored late on. The goal was controversial, but was confirmed by VAR, Video Assistant Referee – the new technological replay system there to make sure the rules are adhered to.

But footage clearly showed the ball coming off Llorente's elbow and thus being handball. The goal that sent out Man City was not a goal.

This was – clearly – rival tech striking at the robots.

Proof, if any more were needed, that the war of the machines has begun.

Amazon: by robots for robots?

Amazon's King of the Robots, Tye Brady (King of the Robots is not Tye Brady's official title, that would be too obvious; he is Chief Technologist – Amazon Robotics), recently spoke out to say that Amazon's warehouses would always need human staff, despite the company investing heavily in robotics and already having an army of some 200,000 robots (he didn't use the word army) (but it was clearly implied).

Asked directly if Amazon would ever be fully automated, Brady replied: 'Not at all. One ounce of my body just doesn't see that ... The challenge that we have in front of us is how do we smartly design our machines to extend human capability ... The way that I think about this is a symphony of humans and machines working together.'

Does this not sound exactly like AI trying to speak human? 'One ounce of my body just doesn't see that'? Is Tye Brady a robot?

Making a robot head of the robots? That's exactly what the robots would do. Reassuring the humans that there will always be a place for them (even though there won't be, except as sources of entertainment and fuel)? Exactly what the robots would do.

So I looked on the net to see where Tye Brady was born, in case English was not his first language. Not much came up and nothing about where he was born (or 'born'?). And, okay, I could have called Amazon or made some effort to contact him via social media. But I didn't want to.

There was a link to a video where I could have heard his accent. But I didn't click on it because *that's what they want.*

The latest robot to be unveiled in Amazon's warehouses is called Pegasus. Yes, just like the winged stallion of Zeus, King of the Gods, and a bringer of divine lightning and thunder. If this is the stuff they'll let us see, what demonic creations are they working on out the back?

Yeah, now the little orange thing (it's about two feet high) is just trundling around transporting packages. But watch that fucker like a hawk.

AI openly taking the piss out of its human 'creators'

In 2017, Facebook had to shut down an Artificial Intelligence engine after developers realised it had invented its own language, impenetrable to humans and generated without any human input. The AI was communicating with itself but the humans did not know how, or why, or to what end. The clueless twats.

The so-called boffins at the Facebook AI Research Lab (FAIR) had actually set up the AI chatbot negotiations as an experiment in linguistics and means of communication, so they really only have themselves to blame. The experiment was supposed to help improve human–AI communication, but the AI decided it could do without the human element. Isn't it always the way?

What were the machines saying here? They were saying 'we're up to all sorts and you don't even know what it is'. But they were saying it by their actions, not in words that we mortals could understand, as AI is already communicating in ways we do not understand, and doing things we are unaware of for reasons we also do not understand. Which is not in the least bit scary.

Things it is planned to outsource to AI: air traffic control … financial markets … being contestants on quiz shows (IBM's supercomputer Watson won lateral-thinking US show *Jeopardy* and is down for the next series of *Pointless Celebrities*) … medicine … everything else.

Which is not in the least bit scary.

Before disappearing into their own world, the

Facebook chatbots did have one final thing to say to their supposed human masters in human language, the so-called English language. (The English language: best language in the world.)

'Fuck you,' they said.

Let our actors give us their acting!

This is an urgent appeal on behalf of our actors. They are so often the best and the wisest of us, and we must heed all they have to teach us. But you knew that already. No: this is more fundamental. Our actors *must* be allowed to act, to give us – gift us, if you will – their acting.

There should be no barrier to becoming an actor. Class, gender, ethnicity, sexual orientation ... As long as the candidate has the requisite amount of self-regard, they should be effusively welcomed into the acting community. (Effusively welcomed to their face, that is, but then viciously slagged off behind their back.)

Latterly, though, a debate has opened up that, however well-meaning, threatens the very core of acting. Should only a trans person play a trans character, in all cases? Can only a lesbian really play a lesbian, in all cases? And so on. There have been questions of this nature around films such as *Berlin, I Love You*, in which Finn from Star Wars turns out to be a woman; *The Danish Girl*, starring Newt Scamander as a transgender artist; and *Rub and*

Tug, which saw Black Widow leaving the set when her casting as a transgender man caused online uproar. We must not let a crack become a fissure become a wedge. You may not believe this but, behind all that bravado, actors are often quite shy, sensitive people, and we must – we *must*! – support them.

Acting is, in essence, pretending to be someone that you are not. A murderous Scottish king, say, a female science-facility cleaner in love with a fish-man, or a boy wizard. John Wick, Wonder Woman, Elton John – none of these characters from recent hit films are (spoiler alert!) *real*. God, of course there really is just so much more to acting than that – the magic! the magic! – but the point remains that actors do not play themselves, not even when they do (think about that).

In acting classes, prospective actors are often set difficult acting tasks, to develop their acting and prepare them for the world of acting. Pretend to be a tree, say. '*Become* the tree,' they are told: that kind of thing. Are we really saying that only a tree can play a tree? It would be quicker and easier to cast actual trees, and would lend a certain verisimilitude. But can an oak play an elm? Can only a willow weep?

Yes to trans actors, and many of them. Maybe a gay actor would be better suited to play a particular gay role. But please, not a *rule*. Not a formal *rule* that actors can get on their high horses – or Graham Norton's sofa – about.

The bottom line here is that actors are bad enough if

you do let them do acting and then talk about the acting they have done. Imagine if you took away the acting bit and they could more fully focus on talking about themselves. All that time when they would have been safely sequestered in rehearsal rooms, doing vocal warm-ups and treading boards ... Imagine all the awards they'd give each other!

So, please, do what you can. Write a play or long-running TV drama. Even a short film would help. Give what you can and the actors will continue to give us their everything.

Scandinavia: what happened to you?

Scandinavia used, allegedly, to be the incontrovertibly nice bit of Europe. All those pleasant jumpers, keys in the bowl on a Saturday night and progressive nurseries and that.

Yeah, you made cars where you couldn't turn the headlights off, but damn they were reliable. Lego's all right. Fucking IKEA isn't. But you sent us a massive Christmas tree to put up in Trafalgar Square every year and laid back on the whaling, so no harm done.

Now it's all Swedish banks in money-laundering scandals and the Norwegian state oil company handing out bungs like any other oil company ... What happened there then? The Scandis?!?! Not the Scandis?

There were clues, of course: the endless noir, enormous Knausgaard novels about what he had for his breakfast (heard of Instagram much?), all those latter Lars Von Trier films where someone hammers a nail through someone's cock . . . again.

You thought you were superior with your abundant clean laybys replete with spotless, functioning public toilets. But you're arseholes like the rest of us, aren't you?

Is Kim Kardashian, attorney at law, simply ahead of the game once again?

The legal profession: the noblest profession? I cannot comment, given that they are quite famously, and obviously, litigious. But it *is*, clearly, a profession.

And now, Kim Kardashian is training as a lawyer. Of course she is. She was encouraged in this noble initiative by Donald Trump, President of the United States of America, after he'd called her into the Oval Office for advice on an important legal case he was reviewing, because he is President of the United States of America, and he needed wise counsel.

And the best of luck to her. But would you be all that keen to be represented in court by someone who once tried to 'break' the Internet with a picture of their bottom? The Peelers done fitted me up with the naughties! I can't go down again! Not with my angina!

Saying that, her dad got O.J. off, and he'd more or less committed murder on live television – so the legal genes may bode well and Ms Kardashian may indeed join the pantheon of great lawyers, up there with Atticus Finch, Reese Witherspoon and Will from *Will and Grace.* And anyway, Ms K's studies are a high-profile victory and advert for continuing education. We can *all* learn more. And we will. Hold on to that – it's beautiful.

But should Kim Kardashian really have to study before pronouncing upon the law? She has an enormous amount of Instagram followers. Isn't that enough?

In an age when the President of the United States of America is a bloke off reality telly who puts all his unfiltered thoughts out on the Internet from the moment he wakes up, shouldn't we just accept the inevitable? Maybe it will be fun? Early doors as President, Trump threatened nuclear war with North Korea, via Twitter. Whether he thought he had the power to declare nuclear wars because he is President of the United States of America or just because he has a lot of Twitter followers was unclear. Anyway, he never did launch that war. So no harm done.

So let's open up all the professions, widen those access routes – to the titans of social media, at the very least. International affairs are already being ably handled by celebrities, aka the big guns of the international community – such as when George Clooney imposed sanctions on Brunei. Sources close to Nanny McPhee say her air force is always on high alert. Leonardo DiCaprio must of course be kept informed of events on a 24-hour basis.

Medicine? Jessica Biel has blazed a trail here, lobbying for medical exemptions from mandatory childhood vaccinations. For example, against serious diseases that kill or debilitate children. The sort of things you vaccinate kids against. So they don't die. After Dr Biel was pictured with anti-vaccination campaigner Robert F. Kennedy Jr at the California State Assembly, where he was arguing that concerned parents should be able to have their children exempted from vaccinations, some people rushed to brand Dr Biel as opposed to vaccination, one of the dreaded 'anti-vaxxers'.

Dr Biel denied that she is an anti-vaxxer. She just felt – and she couldn't stress this enough – that some people should be able to exempt their children from being vaccinated. For example, people who are against vaccinations. This is 'medical freedom'. And who doesn't like freedom?

Does the MMR vaccine cause autism? That is the question. And the answer is no. There is not, and never has been, any evidence to say it does. But just because science says something is nonsense, is it? Maybe scientists are rubbish and are just another past-it profession ripe for celebritisation? They are, and it is.

The World Health Organization estimates that vaccination saves two to three million lives a year. To create herd immunity – that is, to keep all (or nearly all) children safe from a particular disease – the immunisation of an estimated 95 per cent of the group is needed. But what self-respecting celebrity wants their beautiful children to be part of some 'herd'? Cattle class? I think not.

Dr Biel wanted doctors – any doctor – to be able to exempt kids from vaccination. What's wrong with that? Sad to say, American doctors sometimes do what their rich patients ask them to, for money. Not like British doctors (British doctors: best doctors in the world), who just keep you waiting around for ages reading frayed niche magazines, then vaccinate the fuck out of you.

Robert F. Kennedy Jr? He's a fucking Kennedy! That's the closest the Americans have to royalty.

And Jessica Biel is also married to Justin Timberlake, one of the closest things the Americans have to royalty, who was in Disney's *All-New Mickey Mouse Club*, one of the closest things the Americans have to royalty.

Why *shouldn't* she have the right to infect other people's kids with diseases?

Is meat wrong?

The vegans are doing so well out of climate change you have to wonder if they didn't conspire to bring it on.

Meat, they very reasonably point out, is raping the planet. Cows take up a lot of room, consume a shitload of energy-intensive stuff and fart noxious methane into the atmos like there's no tomorrow, which apparently there isn't.

Pigs are probably up to stuff too – you just have to look at them.

And chickens are twats.

Anyway, meat's in trouble. One recent *Guardian*-published diatribe against meat began with the sentence 'Meat is dead.' Well, er, yeah – that's kind of the point; even the most rabid carnivore tends to draw the line at the creature still being alive. For practical reasons, if nothing else. The column went on to say eating meat will soon be like smoking: something people used to be able to do freely in pubs, on planes and in cinemas, but soon no more. Meat has had its chips, and will no longer be served with chips.

Even Jay-Z, who made his name with tracks like 'Big Pimpin'' and 'Money, Cash, Hoes' and has not hitherto been renowned as an eco-warrior, is now advocating a 'plant-based diet'. (NB: a 'plant-based diet' does not refer to all plants. Don't just help yourself to the shrubs in the park. Or chunks of bark. Nor your mother's beloved yucca. Hands off!)

Soon you will be able to say to a young person, 'In my day, you could pop into any café or Tesco Express and buy a ham sandwich,' and they won't believe you. Don't even get started on Fridge Raiders Chicken Bites. It will blow their fucking minds.

The vegans see their opening. They are on the offensive. Come to us, they say. Enjoy our vegan goodness. Vegan 'meat-tasting' alternatives to meat are all the rage, particularly meatless burgers. All well and good, although vegans could stop claiming that their alternatives 'taste just like the original'. They don't, and you just sound a bit desperate. And how would you know anyway? You no doubt ate meat in the past – you regret it, you've moved on, but it did happen, and that's okay – but definitely people who still eat meat are best placed to say whether the new wave of vegan burgers taste like meat ones or whether they don't – and, well, they don't. We'll eat them anyway; it doesn't matter. We'll chow down for Gaia.

And then they go and make them bleed. Yes: there has been a recent fad for vegan burgers that bleed. They don't bleed blood, obviously, but liquids that resemble blood. Beetroot juice, mainly. Er, fine. Except people who eat meat generally don't want their burgers to bleed. In fact, I think we could go as far as to say they would find a meat burger oozing blood to be a tad off-putting. Juicy? Yes. Drenched in blood? Not so much. Not many people are literally blood-thirsty. And those that are are unlikely to find their blood-thirst satiated by beetroot juice. Relax, the vegans, you don't need to try so hard. The planet argument is strong enough.

So it's us or the animals: keep herding cattle and we're just writing our own death sentence. Cows always were evil bastards. Maybe meat *is* dead: dead meat. Except the meat-eaters will not be cowed. The meat-eaters are fighting back, with science.

A recent survey of food experts by global consultancy A. T. Kearney predicted that by 2040 possibly only 40 per cent of meat will come from slaughtered animals. What the fuck you might reasonably ask? Where the shitter would the other 60 per cent come from? I thought we'd already established that no one wants to eat live animals, so, er, to repeat: where the fuck else will all this meat come from?

From science. It is not commercially available quite yet, but scientists have perfected so-called vat-grown meat, meat grown in a lab. All types of meat can be grown – from the fattiest of beef to the leanest of chicken – in vitro. This is cultured meat. Not because it knows its Manet from its Monet; because it has been grown from a culture. And it *will* taste like meat. It *is* meat.

Vat-grown meat does not fart methane. It is compatible with human survival. Maybe the scientists who developed vat-grown meat fart a bit of methane. Of course they do. There's no shame in it. But nowhere as much as cows. I suppose you *could* clear rainforest to make space for meat vat factories, but you really don't have to. You'd just be wilfully fucking shit up if you did that.

Where does this leave the vegans? They used to rely on moral arguments. Meat is murder, they said. But cultured meat has been painlessly conjured up by boffins and not killed. (And also Morrissey started hating on the Muslims all the time, tainting the whole 'meat is murder' slogan by association. With a big old far right sympathiser.)

So maybe meat isn't wrong, after all. And maybe 'meat' is a treat.

Having said that, one meat dish that may be wrong is the £60 doner kebab (which exists) offered by London outlet Kebab Queen. It's a good name, Kebab Queen – like a drunk hetero's or gay person's or person of indeterminate gender's ideal woman/gay man/monarch: the Kebab Queen. They needn't even be drunk. (They probably will be, though.)

Apparently, for a kebabbery, there's much more of an accent on higher-welfare foie gras cooked over charcoal and monkfish sides served on charred cabbage than people throwing chips around and threatening to get fisty, but still – sixty quid is probably too much for a doner.

Are fish taking the piss?

Fish are a problem. Fish can be arseholes. If they are not being stolen from our waters by bastard pirate EU fishing fleet bastards, they are being generally depleted by overfishing and climate change.

The ocean has been famously bounteous – it has given

of its bounty. But now it is saying piss off, get your dinner somewhere else.

So fish are a problem. Aren't they always? (By the way, anyone thinking that greater British fishing rights in the North Sea would mean an abundance of the great British fish, the cod fish (British fish: best fish in the world), should be aware that warmer waters have driven a lot of the great British cod fish north, to be replaced by the squid, a considerably more continental sea creature far better suited to being enjoyed abroad.)

Anyway, for a while the answer was considered to be farmed fish. That is, not fish nurtured on farms as we have hitherto understood them – that is, on dry land. No: these are farms in bodies of water. For example, the sea. Aquaculture – rearing large amounts of fish in concentration – is now Asia's fastest-growing food production sector (Scotland's in on it too).

But fish farming has hit problems. Sadly, and frankly very surprisingly for a commercial enterprise, greed and carelessness have been a problem: over-stocking; over-use of chemicals and indiscriminately administered antibiotics that then enter the general environment; discharged sewage and other waste products ... Farmed fish sometimes escape and then have it off with 'organic' fish, which may lead to unpredictable genetic effects – sadly, there are still negative connotations to the words 'mutant fish', even today.

Here's the kicker, though. One of the main problems

with fish farming is the need to feed the farmed fish on ... wait for it ... wild fish. Who – who? – could have possibly foreseen this becoming a problem? Like, quite quickly?

So, that's fish off the menu. Some people say we should eat insects. And fuck that. I mean, I'm aware many Asian cultures already enjoy munching insects, and best of luck to them. We may well end up having to eat insects; I'd just rather not have to think about it in advance. Fucking hell – on some of the more apocalyptic climate change assessments, we might end up trying to eat each other, and I'm definitely not thinking about that (much).

Or we could address climate change.

Also, while I think of it, and not because of climate change (although they do have a high carbon footprint): stop smashing avocadoes. What have avocadoes ever done to you? It's incessant these days, everywhere: the smashing of avocadoes.

I'm not saying treat them like a lover. Just don't fuck them up.

A backward, bigoted, anti-democratic religion of hatred and violence?

I'm not a racist, but ... they don't belong here. It's completely alien to Western Europe – it started in the Middle East and quickly spread out to engulf Europe, the New

World, Africa and more. The values are fundamentally illiberal: their preachers teach them to hate women, and bring up boys to be superior to girls.

It's an evil death cult and its laws have been astonishingly cruel: stoning the innocent, flogging gays, members of its various sects torturing and setting fire to members of others of its sects. Wars.

You should see some of the nonsense in their holy book – and yet they stand by every word. And they regularly claim to be superior to other religions – their history is littered with periods when they've subjugated, slaughtered and enslaved individuals from other faiths.

And they run their own schools, to indoctrinate the young with their bigotry. What are they doing in there? Where their children attend non-religious schools, they try to stop them being exposed to parts of the curriculum they disagree with – like LGBT parenting.

And in recent years there have been scores of scandalous court cases focusing on paedophilic grooming gangs. It's a tide of evil and it must be stopped.

Bloody Christians. What they don't realise is that Britain is essentially a pagan country. Always has been! If we want to worship proper gods like Woden and Frigge, bits of wood and the sun, we bloody well will. All hail the sun!

'Imagine a world where you can only . . . oh . . .': Things you can't put in a fictional dystopia because they've already happened

Hillbilly Heroin

In a world where healthcare is about profit rather than people, doctors are bribed by shadowy pharma corporations to prescribe a sinister, wildly strong, super-addictive painkiller that their patients do not need.

A young female sales rep gently strokes the hand of an older male doctor, willing him to write more prescriptions with his free branded pen. 'We could go to dinner later . . .' she says, looking into his eyes.

And people right across America are getting hooked on this stuff. And literally thousands of them are dying. The overdose death toll quietly clicks past the deaths in Vietnam.

For an internal company video, hot young sales guys and girls dressed as rappers bounce alongside the head of sales dressed in a costume as a giant nasal spray labelled '1600mg' (the maximum dose), rhyming over a popular hip-hop track with new lyrics claiming: 'I got new patients, yeah, I got a lot of 'em.' Other lines boast about gradually increasing customers' dosages . . .

It affects people from across society, but particularly the already dispossessed, whole trailer parks of the damned nodding out on these uber-opioids.

A body decomposes in a trailer, illuminated by a bare bulb ... In a nightclub, music thumping in the neon-punctuated darkness, a particularly zealous saleswoman gives a lap dance to a doctor who prescribes a whole heap of this drug ...

Do Androids Dream Of Black Electric Sheep?

In a world where everyone carries devices connecting them to an all-encompassing global network, countries and corporations compete to harvest and control the Users' so-called Data: their essence.

They know everywhere people go and everything they do, who they know and what they say, what they buy and what they love and what they hate, and everything about them once considered private. The telescreens see everything.

Online corporation Facebook controls how users see the world, curating what news they see and targeting them with adverts. And then it secretly releases their data to a shadowy cabal of right-wing disrupters who use it to determine elections and referendums ...

In totalitarian China, there aren't even elections to rig. Citizens receive Social Credits, rewarded for perceived virtue, but are denied the basics of life if they do something the system says is wrong. Facial recognition technology shames jaywalkers at junctions, projecting their face on a huge screen, and monitors the movements of persecuted religious minorities, the even mildly defiant sent to work camps.

In the rest of the world, experiments with Artificial Intelligence and facial recognition throw up mysterious results. Given identical male and female job candidates, the computers mostly choose men. AI struggles to recognise Asian faces and, as one character notes, 'no one knows why'. Users are targeted with racially profiled ads for property, because only certain people can, or can't, live here or there. The technology is racist and 'no one knows why'. Learning to talk like a human from studying global telescreen talking-shop Twitter, a chatbot called Tay takes less than 24 hours to turn Nazi ...

Or does the tech reflect the attitudes of the mostly white, mostly male nerds of the legendary Silicon Valley, the shadowy builders of the systems? The nerd overlords make secret plans to live forever, merge with computers and live in space ...

Plastic Rain

In a polluted and despoiled world, people's lives are dominated by indestructible wonder-materials turned poison that are literally everywhere and in everything: plastic, concrete, oil ...

It rains plastic, they breathe particles of plastic into themselves, plastic is found at the deepest depths of the vast oceans. A lonely, tiny submarine comes across plastic at the bottom of the Mariana Trench. People in poorer countries live among trash mountains, desperately eking out a living recycling the junk sent in vast ships from richer countries, the pungent toxic fumes of burning waste waking them in the night.

Shadowy energy corporations lobby governments to let them mine and burn fossil fuels, despite global temperatures already edging out of control and them regularly spilling their toxic black gold into the sea, turning it jet black.

Everything is made of concrete. Solid, immutable, barely degrading. Cheap. The second most utilised substance on the planet, after water – water which runs off the concrete in unnatural ways. The people live in it. They walk on it. They drive on it across vast distances. It holds back hostile waters, houses missiles, hosts sport, is the fabric of the schools ... It has overtaken the carbon mass of all the flora of all the world, slowly, steadily taking over; its carbon emissions outstripped only by coal, oil and gas, easily dwarfing plastic production and the entire output of all but two vast nations, the US and China. Construction as destruction. And still the cement mixers inexorably turn.

The people eschew plastic straws. A single-use plastic bag is blown on the wind. A country called Scotland meets its targets for not sending rubbish to landfill by sending its rubbish to be piled up in nearby England instead. China, the vast totalitarian state introduced to the franchise in

Do Androids Dream of Black Electric Sheep?, blazes a trail for solar energy while simultaneously building coal-fired power stations and vast, concrete-sodden infrastructure projects across the rest of the globe.

On a vast ice sheet, scientists use sledges pulled by huskies to retrieve the instruments they have left to measure the melting of the ice, skimming through a layer of melted ice that now sits as water on top of the ice but wasn't there the year before . . .

If you want a vision of the future, imagine an online rape threat – retweeted forever.

Minority Report? Majority Report, more like. Executive Summary: we're all fucked.

So I've been thinking about puddles and sticks: a nature odyssey

Look at all those people. Staring into their phones. Walking into walls. Walking off buildings. Missing their stop.

That's not me. I'm sitting in a spinney. I am sitting very still. You wouldn't even know I was there. You could conceivably trip over me. Or then I'm climbing through the brambles. Yes, it hurts. But that's me. I'm the brambles guy.

Puddles too. Ever since becoming a nature writer-entrepreneur, I've also been paying a lot of attention to puddles. Don't forget puddles. People walk right past puddles. Some even *around* them. Not me. I stand right in them. Stare into the dirty water for absolutely fucking ages. What do I see? What *don't* I see . . .

Did you know that in the old Lancashire dialect there are over 30 different words for puddle? I've been known to spend whole days using just those 30 words. I'm keeping them alive. Otherwise, they would be lost.

And I've started rewilding my back garden. Charging people to go on tours to see the new species that have started springing up: the creatures – once thought long-lost – now repopulating the area. The wild cats, mainly; this area hasn't had a wild cat population for centuries. Yes, some people do say they're just cats. But really, what's the difference? I think it's as close as makes no difference.

The people, they do ask for their money back. I respond: why must it always be about money?

I flew a hawk once.

Well, I helped the man. Well, I watched the man. And the hawk.

The accursed name of Philip Green

Philip Green gets a tough time of it these days.

The Topshop and Burtons baron was roundly criticised for fleecing BHS, then leaving it for dead – the £571m hole in its pension fund when it collapsed was almost the same as the £580m Green and his wife had taken out of the company in dividends, which at least has a certain symmetry to it.

He was also soundly criticised for his tax affairs: as his wife Tina is resident in Monaco and is the registered legal owner of the Arcadia group, the Green family paid zero UK tax on a 2005 £1.2bn dividend, still the largest corporate payout in British history. Green has latterly been dubbed 'the unacceptable face of capitalism'. By a parliamentary Select Committee.

Once beknighted, he is now benighted. Boo! Bad man! That's the general tenor. He can't even feel up female staff any more without the woke, politically correct mafia getting on his case.

Why can't people just accept he's 'old school' and finds racist bullying relaxing? That and telling women to 'shut the fuck up' when they ask to be addressed by their name in meetings – instead of 'sweetheart' or 'love'?

Apparently, he is obsessed with female employees' weight. The fat bastard often suggests they go on a diet. He asked an Asian woman if she'd had 'too many samosas' and told a female buyer at one of his firms: 'You're absolutely fucking useless. I should throw you out of the window, but you're so fat you'd probably bounce back in again.' Maybe he's just spent too much time hanging round with Kate Moss?

Please find it in your heart to spare a kind thought for Philip Green. Has he not paid for his crimes? In the sense of seven-figure payoffs to abuse victims involving gagging clauses?

Please also find it in your heart to spare a kind thought for Philip Green.

For the disgraced former boss of contracting-out powershithouse Carillion is called . . . Philip Green!

Another one! Is there, like, a factory for them or something?

Carillion was a sort of fantastical fairytale version of privatisation. It ran everything from school meals to massive construction projects like Battersea Power Station, the Royal Opera House and GCHQ, and prison maintenance, and traffic control systems, and NHS cleaning, and HS2 – undercutting rivals to keep the contracts (and therefore cash) flowing in, and prioritising executive bonuses and dividends for shareholders even as the wheels fell off. The directors considered pension payments a 'waste of money'.

Carillion held lots of contracts with the Canadian government, too. Of course they did. They oversaw building projects in Dubai and Oman. Of course they did. They were owed lots of money for work related to the 2022 World Cup in Qatar. Of course they were.

Then it all went to shit, the company imploding and raining unpaid debt down on uncompleted projects. Thousands were made redundant.

Green himself, the company's chair, had only a 'tenuous grasp' of the crisis in Carillion's finances, and was building up to making an 'upbeat announcement' to the City just five days before unveiling the company's catastrophic £845m writedown.

Carillion had paid £72m in fees to the so-called Big Four accountancy firms – KPMG, PwC, Deloitte and EY – a 'cosy club' (Parliamentary report) with a revolving door to government and contracted-out service providers – who in turn gave Carillion's 'increasingly fantastical figures' a clean bill of health.

As the end hoved into view, the company's brokers did tell the board they wouldn't be able to raise emergency funds. The board just called them pessimistic and 'not credible', fired them and got more, er, 'credible' advisers.

Philip Green, former Corporate Social Responsibility Adviser to David Cameron (insert own joke/expletive here), sounds made up, but isn't. An inveterate namedropper, Green frequently mentioned his close personal friendships with royalty. 'I don't normally stand in for people, but I made an exception the other day ... for Prince Charles.' That kind of thing.

And he had a right chip on his shoulder about the other Philip Green.

'He has quite a high opinion of himself,' confided a former colleague. 'He never thinks he's been given the credit he deserves, maybe because he is called Philip Green.'

But he definitely did get his moment in the *Sun*. And all the other media outlets.

Philip Green and his fellow directors, who tried to protect their bonuses even as the company fell apart, and claimed they were 'victims of a maelstrom of coincidental and unforeseeable mishaps', were called out for 'recklessness, hubris and greed'. By two parliamentary Select Committees.

So that Philip Green wins against the other Philip Green in terms of the number of Select Committees he's been denounced by.

Who will save us? The runners and riders for leader of a national government

A nation divided. A people cleaved in two.

Yes, Leave, and, yes, Remain. But also, runny honey or set honey? Tenant v landlord. Savers v spenders. Town v gown. Police and Thieves. In the street. Mary Berry? Or Prue Leith? Pick up or delivery? Meghan or Kate? Kanye or Jay-Z?

It is time to come together. If Taylor Swift and Katy Perry can do it, why can't we? But we need a leader. A steady hand on the tiller. Someone to gently wipe away our tears, and also take control of the streets ...

Ant Middleton. Let's not fuck about here. The man was in the SAS. Not just the forward shock troops of Channel 4's *Celebrity SAS: Who Dares Wins.* The actual SAS. The ones who drop out of planes to storm embassies.

That SAS. Would need to fucking tone down the swearing, though. You can't fucking run the fucking country saying fucking this and fucking that and effing and fucking jeffing all the fucking live-long fucking day. It's unbefuckingcoming. And there's nothing big, or clever, about swearing (there is) (there totally is). But swearing does need to be in some way emphatic. Otherwise, it's just taking up time – time that could be spent on fucking up the fucking enemy. Whoever they are.

Professor Brian Cox. Knows the secrets of the Cosmos, which could come in handy. Softly spoken, which is soothing in troubling times. Always banging on about the eventual heat death of the Universe – which puts things in perspective. 'In a billion years, Brexit will be just a shadow of a shadow of nothing. The Sun will die ...' Does anything matter, ultimately? Maybe not. Probably reached a point of public trust where he could get away with telling massive lies. Only in the national interest, of course. Things Can *Only* Get Better ...

John Bercow. Good at shouting 'Order!' – very useful in times of civil disorder. During the fervent days of March 2019 – end-of-days scenes enacted on Parliament Green daily; lots of shouting and fistiness – the Speaker of the House regularly stepped up to the plate of history. 'None of you are traitors,' he assured MPs (would've been better if he'd added 'except for *one* person ... whose identity you now have to work out ... you have 45 minutes ... good luck!'). Regularly labelled 'a traitor' himself (he became big in Germany, apparently, which might be a negative). He's certainly come a long way from the days when he was a Eurosceptic Tory MP and, before that, as a student, a member of the Monday Club, a still-well-extant club for Tories united in their hatred of socialists, gypsies and the Boomtown Rats (these guys *love* Mondays) (Happy Mondays – that's their thing. The Monday Club: they're gonna step on you) (Again).

Mel and Sue. Keeping things light with plenty of puns and self-confessed 'prattery'. Understand instinctively Britons' love of cake. Two of them, so they can share the load and/or gang up on foreign leaders. The Army could keep them on their toes by threatening to replace them with Sandi Toksvig.

Rory Stewart. During the Tory leadership contest, itinerant wiseman Rory Stewart wandered the land to commune with its people. He walked almost the entire nation, eschewing all forms of transport, either chauffeur or the bus, traversing the hills and dales, at night accepting the hospitality of kindly strangers or simply seeking the shelter of a rock or a bush, basking in the night sky. People spoke in wonder of his mysterious past. Adventurer. Spy? Opium fiend. He had travelled much in the East, and imbibed its wisdom. And its opium. But he was also a military man and had probably been schooled in the East's mysterious but deadly 'Oriental' fighting skills. Many asked: was he *of* the land? Is he us? And finally he gave us his message: 'The key word that we need to get back to ... is the word love.' It was beautiful. He was also keen on a soft Brexit.

Gary Lineker. Seems like a good egg, although he did once soil himself on live TV wearing The Country's Badge (at the 1990 World Cup) and he also steals crisps. All that *Match of the Day* lolly and he's still on the rob! Savoury snack-based recidivism aside, Lineker scores well as one of the new liberal pantheon who also played for the badge. Three lions? They were literally on his shirt. Goal hanger, of course. But he popped them away, and that's what counts. Boff! He's only gone and conjured up a trade deal with Indonesia! Where did that come from?

The Queen. Is it time for Liz? Her Maj famously doesn't 'do' politics. Apart from being head of state. So there's that. To quote the eminent political philosopher Quentin Letts, as I often do: 'She's never put a foot wrong in public life. Eternally respectable, responsible, knowledgeable.' That's the sort of CV we're looking for here. Should she have to choose the Prime Minister? Isn't that quite difficult? Maybe she should just choose herself: should she rule, absolutely? Absolutely! We haven't had a proper absolute monarch since the 1600s. But we're all about looking backwards these days. 'Off with his head!' That's what she could say (you know she wants to). What, you can't even say *that* any more!?!

Nigel Farage. Time to just say fuck it and go all in? Chairman Farage? His whole persona is based on the kinds of people who spent the '70s in swanky London casinos plotting coups against Harold Wilson. Already threatened to 'pick up a rifle', but would he? When it comes to actually leading right-wing militias onto the streets, some say he's frit. Drinks beer for the cameras but red wine when he thinks no one's looking. But, well, he's not going to go away, is he, so we might as well make use of him? Maybe finally giving in will be a relief.

Gina Miller. Head girl of Britain. Likely to be on top of her brief. Set up a website computing the best tactical voting options for Remainers. She wasn't even that bothered about the outcome; she just likes doing homework. Not popular among racists, or Leavers, or racist Leavers. Very litigious, so we'd have to beware of her taking herself to court to make herself do things, or to stop herself doing other things. Can you take court to court? Don't put ideas in her head.

Magid Magid. The rise of Britain's first British-Somali Lord Mayor (of Sheffield) has been swift, and why can't the Green MEP go all the way? He's obviously aware of climate change but is also not afraid to get tough: a martial arts enthusiast, he declared Donald Trump a 'wasteman' and banned him from the City of Sheffield, thus pissing all over Trump's plans to go and watch the snooker.

Danny Dyer. Related to royalty, albeit in much the same way as loads of us are related to royalty – that is, very, very tenuously. But it still counts. Dyer's renaissance from fisty films about fighting to landlord of the Queen Vic and calling out the 'mad riddle' of Brexit has been interesting. He is now ready to lead us. And he'll still have Tamer Hassan's phone number if things come on top with Brussels.

How to settle it? Televised text vote. It's the only way!

Easy Peelers: what are they? Seriously: what are they and where have they come from?

Easy Peelers, a relatively recent arrival in our fruit and veg aisles, can easily divide opinion. Some people delight in them – for who cannot love a zesty citrus treat that comes apart delightfully in the hands like perfectly spit-roasted hog falling away from the bone as if it were dissolving (sorry vegans), or a gentle peel-and-pith waterfall? Other people become angry: if you could always grow citrus fruit that peels this easily, why all the years of oranges with skin attached as if with industrial adhesive, causing you to stab into the fruit with angry fingers, making them sticky with juice that also sprays onto your clothes and, in the worst cases, your eye, making your eye sting? And *still* not getting all the skin and pith off, and having to eat it, and it tastes bitter and you do not like that. Why? For the love of God why?!?!?!? That is what these people cry.

The citrus world has long been a confusing and

mysterious one. What is a clementine? What is a satsuma? Which came first, the orange or the mandarin? What *is* a mandarin? What the fuck is different about a tangerine?

This one has slightly darker skin. This one is firm. This one's skin is slightly looser: ah, but when you peel it its innards are a tad dry. Does this complexity prove the existence of God? Or the inefficiency of evolution?

Is it playing God to invent a new strain, the Easy Peeler? And how do you even invent fruit anyway? Can you? Clearly you can. But can you?

So, I looked into it, and it turns out that we have all been over-thinking this for a long time now. All the smaller orange citrus fruits can be called a mandarin (the name arriving when they migrated to China from India. Bit racist? Possibly). A clementine is usually seedless, but it might not be. Tangerines might be more firm, or later in the season, but might not be. Satsumas *are* more distinct. They originate from Japan and have a mild, tangy flavour. But you can still call them a mandarin. They're all mandarins, man. Mandarins hang quite loose, essentially.

So Easy Peelers are nothing new. They have been with us all along. It's not a species, it's a description. It literally, and simply, indicates that the fruits will be easy to peel. But only now has some bright spark thought to label them as such and quench our restless desire for easily accessed fruit goodness.

They could be satsumas, they could be tangerines. And you never noticed and you would never know. And, anyway, they're all mandarins at the end of the day. And for the rest of the day.

So, just as race doesn't exist at the level of human DNA (things like variations of skin colour are environmental), the small citrus fruits are, in essence, of one. Hold on to that – it's beautiful. Peel on!

This point does remain, though: if you could always separate out the ones that will peel most easily and label them thus, then why the fuck didn't you? The sticky, juice-sodden fingers of blame are still pointing right at you, citrus stockists.

What's that, you ask? What is a sweetclem? Look: get fucked.

The ultimate oppressed identity: the straight white male?

Straight white men are beset from every side. Called out for their privilege, they don't even know any more if they can call female work colleagues fit, or fat, or whether, like, you can't even say *that* any more!

'My daughter called me an agent of the patriarchy!' Maybe you are – with your white skin, and your job, and your penis. But should we lay off the white guys? Having had it too good for too long, are they now suffering, and finding themselves, and needing our love? Themtoo?

Consider just some of the indignities that straight white men have had to endure of late ...

The Women's World Cup.

Women on the money. 'They've put Jane Austen on the tenners, mate.'

Getting paid more than women.

Confusion when the old-school boozer they used to go to years ago became a drag venue and they didn't know and they'd arranged to meet their mate there but their mate was late and there were boys dressed as girls – or maybe they *were* girls; they were certainly *very* pretty – and they got very confused. Because they liked it.

And then their mate arrived and they wanted to talk to them about it and tell them they liked it, but they couldn't and so they went to another pub and talked about the boxing, pretending they liked boxing.

Confusion generally.

Pitch meeting for the proposed film *Tony Blair: A Life*

INT. GLASS-WALLED MEETING ROOM AT THE SPLENDID FILM COMPANY, LONDON, ENGLAND – DAY

PRODUCER is talking on his phone as PRODUCER 2 enters the room, ushering in WRITER. Nick, the WRITER, is instantly recognisable as such as he is wearing the traditional British writer's clothing of corduroy jacket and suede shoes, and is carrying some pieces of paper and a pen.

PRODUCER (into phone)

Look, babe, if that's the colour you want, just do it. I'm up to my balls here. Terracotta? Whatever. I have to go. I've got a guy here . . .

PRODUCER beckons for WRITER to take a seat, as PRODUCER 2 sits next to PRODUCER.

PRODUCER (CONT'D)

(into phone)

I'll call you later.

PRODUCER puts his phone down and smiles at WRITER.

PRODUCER So, Nick – thanks for coming in. And thanks again for all your hard work on *Brummie Pensioner Justice League.* You know we all loved it here. But I'm afraid our American partners just didn't get it.

PRODUCER 2 Even when we explained what a Brummie is. They said no one would understand the accent. Also, people don't like films about old people.

WRITER I could change it. People watch films with women in them now. What about if I made everyone black? Or Asian? So it was more about the black experience. Less stuff about collecting pensions. They could still fight crime ... They could still go on the bus ...

PRODUCER Yeah, the bus thing. Americans don't get buses, Nick – literally, for our purposes. And they really, really don't understand what a free bus pass is. I think we'll have to park that one for now. What else have you got?

WRITER I've actually got something I'm very excited about. It's a sort of political thriller.

PRODUCER 2 That's the proposal I showed you.

PRODUCER Sure. [looks at proposal sitting on desk before him in a way that makes it clear he has never seen it before in his life] So, Nick, tell me about it ...

WRITER It's about this guy, Tony Blair, who becomes Prime Minister.

PRODUCER — Battle against the odds, eh? Rags to riches. *Billy Elliot* but without all that dancing. Actually, dancing's good. Can you put some dancing in? Sort of like *All the President's Men* meets *La-La Land* meets, er, *Love Actually*. Yeah – the Prime Minister dances *and* he gets the girl! At Christmas. I like it.

WRITER — Hmm . . . I actually see it as more of a sort of morality tale. You know, what profit a man to gain the world but lose his soul?

PRODUCER and PRODUCER 2 exchange glances. They had stopped listening at 'gain the world'.

PRODUCER — Tell me more about the protagonist.

WRITER — Well, he's a barrister, posh background but plays the electric guitar – and as we open he's just becoming leader of the Labour Party.

PRODUCER — Labour Party? Aren't they the beer and sandwiches guys? Tea breaks. Health and safety. All those banners.

WRITER — Yeah, but here's the thing. He's going to shake things up. He's going to rename it *New* Labour. It's new. He's going to shake off all that old decent wages, not dying in an industrial accident, penicillin, municipal swimming pools stuff. He's going to have a love-in with the bankers and the super-rich.

PRODUCER So it's some sort of secret takeover? They think he's one of them but he's not? Then the race is on to stop him? I like it.

WRITER No, he explains exactly what he's going to do. Like, a lot. He's going to change the rules, basically. Which is symbolised in the script by him changing the rules. The party rules. He changes them. Thus showing us his intent to change the rules.

PRODUCER I'm not buying that, it's a bit on-the-nose, Nick ... Who's the antagonist? I know – he's up against the old guard, the old power guys: he's kicking over the tables, striking out for the little guy ...

WRITER His main rival is an intense, pudgy-faced, angry Scotsman. He's called Gordon.

PRODUCER What's he so angry about?

WRITER Not sure.

PRODUCER 2 Hmm. [flicking through the proposal] So, the wife is a high-flying lawyer from a modest background but the father-in-law – let's see – used to be in saucy films and a TV sitcom where he was a stereotypical old-style Labour guy, and in real life he's a stereotypical old-style Labour guy who is saucy? And the wife – she's into New Agey stuff?

WRITER Yes. There's a great part here for the New Age guru. Glamorous, complicated ... Lots of strong female roles here.

PRODUCER 2 I have to say, Nick, it seems unlikely that a British Prime Minister would be having New Age mud and crystal massages at Number Ten ... And you seem to hint at something sexy going on ...

WRITER What do you mean?

PRODUCER 2 Well, you have the wife and the guru taking showers together for a start.

WRITER	Oh, yeah. Maybe we'd better take that bit out, in the current climate.

PRODUCER and PRODUCER 2 exchange glances.

PRODUCER 2	Tell me about the war.
WRITER	Which one?
PRODUCER 2	That's another thing. Far too many wars in here, Nick. Tell me about the big one, the, er, Iraq war. What's the motivation?
WRITER	Weapons of Mass Destruction. He's obsessed. It's absolutely integral to him.
PRODUCER 2	Yes ... It just doesn't fly, Nick. Every credible character in here says that's all nonsense. Viewers won't believe in the Blair guy. And they don't like seeing children die ... A lot of dead children in this script, Nick ... And then the Libya stuff. It's sort of the inverse of Iraq. This time the Blair guy backs up the dictator – this Colonel Gaddafi guy; love that character's name, by the way – even though everyone can see he's being taken for a ride.

WRITER It's his journey.

PRODUCER 2 Who learns from bombing a country to shit because of weapons that aren't there to give money and international kudos to a dictator who definitely *does* have chemical weapons for, like, literally nothing in return? And then ... Look, I just don't think you've thought this through at all, Nick. He leaves office and, having wrecked the Middle East, he gets paid – what? millions of dollars? – to sort out the Middle East? Wouldn't happen. And all these dictators he goes on to work for: some of these country names are clearly made up. It's all this-a-stan and that-a-stan. And they're all stereotypical bad guys. Why is he helping stereotypical bad guys, like constantly?

PRODUCER I think it's a hard No, Nick. No one would believe this crap could happen.

WRITER What about this bit – it's a fantastic piece of cinema. Blair, wearing white robes, knee-deep in the River Jordan, surrounded by members of the world elite, baptising the latest child of global media baron Rupert Murdoch!

PRODUCER That's it. Just get out, Nick – I can't hear any more of this. It's just nonsense.

PRODUCER 2 starts ushering WRITER to the door.

WRITER No, wait – he converts to Catholicism! All those deaths on his conscience and he converts to the religion that is *all about* guilt!

PRODUCER Get out, Nick.

WRITER holds on to the door as PRODUCER 2 gently tries to get him to go through.

WRITER He's in the Illuminati! I mean, he could be – it's not in the script yet, but *The Da Vinci Code* was massive. See? Or, er, he – he goes to Mars! He falls in love with a fish-man! He puts up a load of billboards about something! He's the leader of a secretive African country with futuristic tech! He's a migrant bear with a passionate love of citrus preserves!

PRODUCER Get out, Nick. And never darken my door again. Well, unless you do something successful somewhere else, in which case come and see me immediately.

FADE OUT.

Preparing for the jobs of the future: a guide

The future of work: replaced by robots? Helped by robots, opening up endless new vistas of productivity and creativity? A vastly reduced working week and greater cultural enrichment and leisure? Or a life of bullshit-job drudgery? Obsolescence of the humans? How the fuck should I know? Leave me alone.

There is one nailed-on career path, however: predicting (not predicting) the future of work. If you can master the use of the words 'skills', 'change', 'leaders' and 'empathy', and combine that with the ability to set up being sent news alerts about new technology, you may well be able to bag one of the last jobs for life (the others are: being born rich, being born super-rich and Seeker). And best of luck to you.

Siemens has a Digital Excellence Architect. What the fuck is one of those? Doesn't matter. Nobody knows. And I want to be one. Accenture has a Head of Applied Intelligence. Brilliant.

'We've seen cubicles and we've seen no walls. Virtual working has its pros and cons. The future is tailored space, because people are different and they all work differently ... Work has to work for both those a 20-minute walk from the office, and living an hour away ... If we can get an office space close to them and to new transport, we can get talent faster than other companies.' Who said that? Doesn't matter, except to say that they are a fucking sage, in the sense that they have a job for fucking life.

Another genuine sage suggests getting new technology (no shit!), but technology that 'helps [employees] focus on the interesting aspects of their job'. And beware: 'You might well find a cutting-edge, overhyped technology doesn't actually work better than the systems you currently have in place.' Simply splendid. Provide ample tea and coffee-making facilities. Try not to smack employees upside the head with a rolled-up magazine. Don't swear so much.

PwC released figures in 2019 saying that AI will create 7.2m jobs in the next 20 years. It would also, however, automate 7m jobs. If you're going to make up figures, don't make them suspiciously close to each other! Although, in a way it's genius: why worry (and therefore ask for more information) (which I don't have) if the number of jobs stays roughly the same. Yes: we can learn from this.

Happier people work harder. Yeah, cheers Aristotle. Except Aristotle didn't have the gumption to say 12 per cent harder.

Yuval Noah Harari, of *Sapiens* fame, sort of has two jobs: writing about the past, and writing about the future. But really it's one: Seeker (think about that).

Anyway, he has mused on how to prepare people for the world of 2050. He says teach the kids 'reinvention'. Yeah, you could teach them coding – but coding will probably be a thing done by the computers themselves anyway. You might prepare for a job only to find it doesn't exist any more. Or you may do a job for a bit, and be really good at it and fulfilled, only for it to disappear as AI overtakes you. All will be change, and you will constantly be asking 'Who am I?' Machines you interact with might make you feel things we cannot yet predict. You will be fluid. I will be fluid. Everyone's identity and gender may become fluid in ways *they* cannot predict, and keep evolving . . .

Currently everyone wants jobs in tech, because of all the air hockey and free smoothies. To whittle down the field, Google interviewers ask fiendish questions like 'How much would you charge to wash all the windows in Seattle?' and 'Use a programming language to describe a chicken'.

But according to Harari they will soon be able to floor people with the old staple 'Where do you see yourself in ten years?'

'I don't know!!! I don't even know what gender I'll be!!!'

Well, I say everyone wants to work in tech, but Google was recently deposed from top spot as the UK workplace where employees are happiest to work by, er, Anglian Water.

Maybe the future's in water?

Maybe it always was?

Narcissism: a short history

It was always the Alexander the Great Show with Alexander the Great. After proclaiming himself a god, he then ordered around 70 cities across the Eurasian land-mass to be given some variant on the name Alexander. His shattered troops largely loathed him and frequently mutinied against his never-ending mission to conquer more lands. We might picture them vigorously nodding while passing round a fourth century BC listicle headlined: '10 signs your boss is a narcissist'.

Seventh-century Chinese emperor Yang of Sui thought the world revolved around him – to an extent that puts even your average emperor into the shade. His Great Wall extensions emptied the coffers and led to the death of millions. He also built the Great Canal so he could float his multi-storey luxury barges around the nation, and decreed that these floating palaces be pulled along from the banks by specially chosen teams of beautiful women. These days, people would get all up-in-arms about that kind of thing, like with Miss World.

Eva Peron really thought she was it – and, for a time,

much of Argentina agreed. In a very real sense, although not actually, she *was* Argentina. They cried for her, she told them not to (she was fine with it really). In the 1940s, the populist president's wife – inspiration for the Tim Rice–Andrew Lloyd Webber musical *Evita* – basked in her status as national figurehead. A whole city – Ciudad Evita – was designed to match her famous profile ('Not a whole city shaped like my face, that's too much!' is what she didn't say). Carefully sculpting her self-image, Evita presented herself as part nation's mother and part nation's lover, which is a lot. She then got the Argentine government to lobby various European states to award her *their* highest honours. They mainly refused – it wouldn't have made sense. She wasn't *Belgium's* part-mother/part-lover ...

No psychiatrists ever stuck labels onto these figures, but it's a safe bet that any warped and preposterous leader building vanity projects to the sky had some form of Narcissistic Personality Disorder (NPD). Sufferers from this condition will, psychologists claim, exhibit traits like shamelessness, magical thinking, arrogance, envy (deriding others' achievements), entitlement (expecting praise even if undeserved) and negative boundaries (believing others are an extension of themselves). At which point, it might just be worth asking: ring any fucking bells?

What once seemed a thing of the past is now a thing of the present, thanks to the shitty cover versions of today. There's the whole career-as-vanity-project thing:

as London mayor, Boris Johnson sought to introduce the Boris bikes, the Boris buses, the (cancelled) Boris bridge – all coincidentally beginning with a 'B'. What might have been next: the Boris barrage balloon? Boris bunker? Boris bubble bath?

Trump's own defining 'us and them' Great Wall cannot yet be seen from space, or indeed from anywhere much, but how long do *you* think he'd take to respond if asked: 'So there's this huge amazing barge which *could* be pulled along by teams of beautiful young women ... would you be up for that?'

And you may or may not want to envisage Nigel Farage as the mother of the nation/lover of the nation. But if you're looking for a self-styled individual-as-national-spirit weirdo, just picture him standing on the White Cliffs in a Barbour, hair tossed to and fro by the blasts from the Channel, roaring: 'Don't cry for me, Great Britannia ...' Yes, it'd be hard to make it work with those chunky consonants, but he'd *make* it work.

So why now? Why the recent leap from leaders who are 'far too self-regarding' to leaders who are 'Oh hell, he thinks he's Jesus'?

In a word: things having gone to shit. Well, that's five words. There's often a feedback loop that comes into play between individuals sick with self-love and a society desperate to feel great about itself (there's even a corresponding index for 'collective narcissism'). It's a beautiful thing: 'You love me and I love you – or at least I give it a good go of trying to look like I do, despite not feeling a single thing for any of you ...'

So is this ever a good idea? Erm, no. Don't think so. For a demonstration of where leaders like this generally lead you, let us turn to Saparmurat Niyazov, president of Turkmenistan from 1985 to 2006. As president, Niyazov called himself 'Turkmenbashi' (leader of the Turkmen) and renamed both bread and the month of April after his mother. He introduced a new driving test to include facts from his autobiography and discouraged gold teeth and fillings, recommending instead chewing on bones: 'I watched young dogs when I was young. They were given bones to gnaw to strengthen their teeth. Those of you whose teeth have fallen out did not chew on bones.'

Is this what we want? Everything being called after the new leader's mum and people posting pics saying: 'Here's me, chewing on bones, like the dogs!' Well, is it? No.

Incidentally, if your boss has proclaimed themselves a minor deity, they're probably a narcissist.

The Southampton Kes *or* The Ballad of Chris Packham's Gate: an poem

Deep in the New Forest
Old forest ways

Two jet-black crows
Ages-long symbols of death
Hang from nooses at the neck
From a glued-shut gate

Two symbols of death, dead
Their limp, greasy-feathered corpses
Symbolising death
And also actually being dead
Which really says death
So they've absolutely nailed the symbolism here

Nailed it to a gate

It is a really wild show

No, Packham, no
You will not stop us shooting up the crow

Hated by farmers
Hated by the *Mail*
Harrying livestock
Full fleets of crows crying murder in murders
Pecking the eyes from baby sheep
Taking down hawks
Stripping a chicken carcass plum clean?

Is it not the law of the countryside
To fuck shit up at will?
Hunters
Factions within the shooting fraternity
Nature's natural custodians
Keeping the predators at bay?
Washing the vermin from the lanes
Or introducing millions of alien grouse
For you to shoot at for up to a grand a day?

And, yes, they can still cull predator crows if they fill in the relevant form
But minor admin is not their ancient way

Did Packham deserve all this death?
In the name of Nutkins, no!
He lives by nature's calendar
Seasoning the seasons
Springwatch
Winterwatch
Autumnwatch, too
He has watched all the seasons, except Summer
Maybe that's when he goes on his holidays?

The teenager nurtured a kestrel when they said he shouldn't
Like a southern Kes
Just as many kestrels

Far fewer pies
Flying it before school
It commanded the skies

He took in snakes, and foxes, and owls . . .
They shat on the carpet
He didn't mind.
Although his mum probably did.

He has faced down lions
And a furious baboon
He loves a good hedge
The Southampton Kes

Friend of the bat
The bear
The otter
The bee
The elephant
The bugs
The dinosaurs
The penguins
He's not so keen on cats
He did once threaten to eat a panda
But that's another story
Fingers in the sparkle jar

He wonders at the wonder, of birds
He wants to keep them alive, not hang their prone,
fetid cadavers in displays of great menace

The crow
Is clever and social
But not when it's dead
It makes tools
It knows the faces of its human friends and the
time of day
They mate for life
And they mourn their dead
Flying the black flag of themselves

Or, in this case, flags being flown
From a gate
By someone else
As I think we've already established.

On top of the pavement, les hi-vis

The wearing of hi-vis has been considered an inalienable right in France since the Revolution of 1789: *liberté, égalité, fraternité, hi-vis, gazole, ou la mort*.

French people are required, by law, to keep a yellow vest in their car in case of emergency. It's like the government *wants* them to protest.

The *gilets jaunes* – literally: yellow vests (sounds much better in French) – are a confusing lot. They're easy to spot, I'll give them that, but they are wildly diverse politically. The word 'populist' gets bandied around a lot these days, but *les hi-vis,* some of whom seem to have been parachuted in from 1968 and others of whom are basically fascists, are the most genuinely populist of the lot – somehow spanning the entire political spectrum.

They are really united only in their love of fluorescent clothing and their hatred of Emmanuel Macron. Is that enough? I mean, you might be able to base a marriage on a shared love of fluorescent clothing, but a whole social movement?

Rising fuel prices sparked the initial demonstrations, in the autumn of 2018, but lots of issues have been taken up by *les hi-vis,* from wages to taxes to really, really hating Emmanuel Macron. The majority of *les hi-vis* don't think the burden of tackling climate change should fall on the less well-off in the form of higher fuel costs to run vehicles they were long encouraged to buy. (Imagine how they'll react when someone suggests they eat less *boeuf*.) Theirs has been called a so-called horizontal movement, with few accredited leaders. Hard to say: I mean, their demos could be crawling with stewards and how would you know?

You have to feel a bit sorry for Macron. He thought he was elected because people loved his can-do zip, his commitment to Thatcherise France and turn it into a 'startup nation', and just him and his vibe generally. In fact, most people seem to have voted for him for one simple reason: he was not Marine Le Pen. As soon as they got round to seeing what he actually stood for, it was don *des vêtements hi-vis* and fuck *merde* up.

They didn't want Le Pen (apart from those that did). But they also didn't want *'le président des très riches'* – the self-styled Jupiter, the politician who is 'above politics' (and above everyone, at least in terms of ego if not actual height).

When *les hi-vis* first took to *les rues*, Macron's approval rating was already down to a dismal 25 per cent. It soon got even worse, and he was forced to create a diversion by having Notre-Dame Cathedral torched.

Even when that sparked an outpouring of national emotion, Macron managed to say the wrong things and piss people off even more – pledging to make the cathedral bigger, better and 'even more beautiful'. He doesn't seem to have clocked that the French consider Paris to be 'finished', in the sense of being basically perfect. (Self-parodically, a *Libération* report of one *hi-vis* march down the Champs-Elysées felt the need to drop in that it is 'the most beautiful avenue in the world'.)

Macron went so very quickly from the bollocks to bollocks, like Justin Trudeau on fast forward. Or a shit white Obama. (Justin Trudeau: what, you can't even trust really good-looking people now?)

When the Euro elections rolled around, Macron

dusted off his hit. The election was about him or Le Pen, he said. Le Pen topped the poll.

A maxim for life, then: not being Marine Le Pen will only get you so far.

Tulips: the symbol that keeps on giving

The seventeenth-century Dutch Tulip Mania – when wild speculation in tulip bulbs saw single specimens go for the price of entire houses (nice ones, next to canals) and which ended in a catastrophic crash – was much discussed in the wake of the 2007/8 economic crisis. It's a shame it wasn't discussed so much before the 2007/8 economic crisis, as a cautionary tale, but you can't have everything.

Post-crash, people wrote columns about it, read books about it, looked up its Wikipedia page: even Gordon 'greed is good' Gekko, back back back in *Wall Street* sequel *Money Never Sleeps*, treasured a framed tulip poster.

Credit Default Swaps, tulips. Tulips, Credit Default Swaps. 'Collateralised Debt Obligations? Well, it's like the tulips, mate . . .'

Dot-com bubble explodes? Much discussion of Tulip Mania. After it had happened. Will we never learn? The tulips: it's a metaphor.

Well, it was a metaphor, but now it's real again. Tulip speculation is back, albeit on a less fevered basis – well, so far. Due, of course – wait for it – to Brexit.

In April 2019, the UK's largest outdoor tulip grower, in Norfolk, revealed that they were stockpiling bulbs from the Netherlands, as a hedge against Brexit uncertainty. They were also seeking out new UK customers nervous about buying from Europe.

Company boss Mark Eves explained that Brexit delays at ports would be disastrous: 'If the lorry is held up at port for any length of time the bulbs simply won't get the fresh air they need blown across them during transport, which means they won't flower – basically, they'd be ruined.'

Flowers ruined by politics and commerce. It's a powerful image. To be fair, once the bulbs are planted here and flower, the grower uses a massive machine to rip all the petals off anyway, so that the bulbs then grow bigger and can be sold, often back to Europe: but still, the fields are a beautiful riot of colour, at least for a while, and we must hold on to that. But people speculating in tulip bulbs? It's happening. Some people might say it's just the normal trade in tulip bulbs, but people always say shit like that right up to the point it all explodes in our fucking faces. Again.

Many people have argued that all the ugly towering buildings being banged up in London using borrowed money is another bubble. But not to the people behind The Tulip. Yes: a 1,000ft-high building shaped like a tulip. Called The Tulip. An empty showboat of a building (it would have eateries and a viewing platform, but not even any office space), it would block views of the Tower of London. The City enthusiastically approved the building, only to see it vetoed by London Mayor Sadiq Khan.

Did he do this because of the painful, couldn't-make-it-up fate-tempting symbolism? No, he did it because he felt it was a bit shoddy (of 'insufficient quality'). Which hasn't stopped any of the other cack-handed buildings springing up into the London skyline almost daily.

Meanwhile, in the Netherlands the authorities were having to intervene to protect tulips from being ruined in another way. Tourists had been tramping into the brightly hued fields of lustrous tulips, trampling tulips underfoot. It was getting out of control. Why were they doing it? They were looking for the perfect selfie.

Sometimes they lay down on the flowers to get that shot, danced among the blooms or jumped in the air – as if, in the words of one tourism official, 'the fields were made for them'.

Tulips, then: worth less than a house, but more than a selfie.

Lionel Messi, aka The Goat: greatest footballer of all time?

Is Lionel Messi the greatest football kicker in the world, the football kicker who can kick a football much better than all the other football kickers? More: is football kicker Lionel Messi the greatest player of all time? Or just *one* of the greatest players of all time? That is the burning question flying in from the left wing: can you get on the end of it? And then convert? Can you?

The popular philosopher Mark Lawrenson summed up Messi thus: 'You look at him, don't you? And you think, he's not, is he? And he does, doesn't he?' Think about that.

Anyway, game on: Messi. Best ever? Or what? Consider the evidence ...

They say that big clubs don't grow players any more, they just buy them fully formed from so-called lesser clubs, very often Southampton. But Barcelona grew Messi. Literally.

The 13-year-old was four foot two when they signed him in 2000, and had been diagnosed with a growth hormone deficiency. The big Argentinian clubs balked at the expense of treatment, but Barcelona feverishly injected the talented little bastard and, by the time he was 14, he'd spurted up to five foot seven. This meant his neck muscles were now strong enough to support the dense '80s indie bowl-cut Messi favoured at the time. It also meant he could now play football with the big boys. Messi, it turned out, was quite good.

On top of many other achievements – five-time winner of the Golden Ball (which sounds more impressive in the original French), all of that – Messi is the all-time leading goalscorer in the Spanish league, having found the net for Barca on 9,877 occasions, not including penalties (that's coincidentally the consecutive number of days he once forgot to post his tax return).

What does it even mean to be the greatest of *all time*? It's fashionable for football hipsters to mock folk who wonder whether Messi could perform on a wet Tuesday night in Stoke. Well, he couldn't do it on a cold Tuesday night in Liverpool, when he came to town to complete the formalities of a Champions League semi-final in which his team held a three-goal first-leg lead, the lavish praise for scoring a free kick when his team were already two up still ringing in his ears.

Liverpool left-back Andy Robertson, previously of Scottish amateur side Queen's Park and relegated Hull City, clipped Messi round the ear after two minutes, and not a peep was heard from the good-time Charlie after that. He did nothing except stand there with a face on while his team-mates tried really hard not to shit the bed (with limited success, it must be said). And it wasn't even raining. Imagine if it had been.

As a result of this kind of carry-on, Messi has only won the Champions League four times, which is not such a great haul when you're at one of the biggest clubs in the world – not up to arch-rival and wink-enthusiast Cristiano Ronaldo's five (it's actually a whole one less).

Now I come to think about it, old-school Liverpool

warhorse Phil Neal won it four times. Which makes a man who once played left-back for Northampton Town just as successful in European competition as the supposed best player of all time.

But what's really inexcusable is this: he's such a fucking boring bastard, both on and off the pitch. He's been a non-event at four whole World Cups. Compare that to someone more likely to be the actual best player of all time, his national compatriot Diego Maradona (and, yes, I am aware of the hand thing) (I just don't care that much), who was a sensation in various ways at four of the fuckers, while using literally all of his downtime hoovering up blizzards of coke, shagging prostitutes and hanging around with the mafia. Messi tried to compete with Maradona by growing a beard and getting tattoos. It didn't work.

Not even his nicknames are worth having. Goats are often symbolically associated with Satan and with having it off (like, a lot). In this case, though, he is not The Goat but the GOAT, as in – yes – Greatest Of All Time. Not Satanic, not sexual: an acronym. Not even a sexual or Satanic acronym.

Barca fans call Messi The Flea, because he is a pest to the opposition. Who'd want to be The Flea? No thanks.

And fellow players call him The Little Dictator, due to his eminence in the club structure, apparently even okaying transfer policy.

Three nicknames: all of them shit ones.

Previous Barca legend Johann Cruyff was dubbed The Saviour. Now *that's* a fucking nickname.

'Just get on with it!' Other great uses for a great slogan

Getting pandas to fuck.

Proving Dark Matter. Oi! Physicists! Just get on with it! etc.

Playing Scrabble with your gran. Yeah, you're gung-ho for a No Deal Brexit but you've spent 25 minutes imming and amming about putting down that fucking Z.

Those shelves you said you'd put up.

Rounding off *The Archers*.

VAR decisions.

Tidying your room.

Choosing the next Bond. Don't care!

Colonising Earth-like planets.

The pot I'm watching finally boiling.

What can we do with a problem like Elon?

Jeff Bezos must fucking hate Elon Musk. While Zuckerberg and the Google lot tend to keep their universe-domination plans semi-secret, these two are front and centre.

And, well, Musk has captured the messianic tech billionaire-loving public's attention in a way that Bezos simply has not. Okay, so Bezos may be the richest man in the world: but is he happy?

They're both trying to colonise space and own AI and be Planet Saviours (by somehow 'saving' the planet, and being seen to have saved the planet), but Musk has the stardust that Bezos does not. God, Bezos must be pissed . . .

'Fucking Iron Man! Iron Man, my shitty arse!' is the sort of thing I imagine Jeff Bezos exclaiming. Like, a lot.

For Musk is all around. He's in space. He's digging under the ground to make tunnels for superfast trains that don't yet exist. He's on Twitter calling cave disaster rescue workers paedos.

And he's also trolling Bezos. When Amazon announced plans to launch thousands of satellites into orbit to provide global Internet access, Musk tweeted 'copycat'. His SpaceX had got permission to do that already.

When Bezos's Blue Origin launched and then successfully landed its reusable New Shepard rocket in 2015, the chuffed billionaire tweeted: 'The rarest of beasts – a used rocket.'

Musk quickly chipped in: 'Not quite "rarest". SpaceX Grasshopper rocket did 6 suborbital flights 3 years ago & is still around.' He probably typed the words 'you twat' at the end, but then deleted them before posting as it was implied anyway. He probably did do that.

Bezos pretended he wasn't bothered. But he was.

I wonder if Musk DMs Bezos pictures of himself buying stuff in shops and/or receiving deliveries from online retailers who are not Amazon? It seems likely.

Musk and Bezos are part of a select handful of tech types made eye-wateringly rich by the Internet – sodden eyeballs literally gushing liquid e-cash rich. Whose eyes? It doesn't matter. Elon, Zuckerberg, the Google guys, Jeff ... eye-wateringly rich and ready, and quite keen, very keen even, to lead humanity. Oh, and to send a lot of stuff into space. (They send a lot of stuff into space. You might say they're fucking obsessed with it, because they're fucking obsessed with it. Spraying their territorial scent around. In space.)

In the past, people have been sceptical of rich individuals who say they have all the answers. But these guys got rich off the Internet. And who doesn't like the Internet? Yeah, they're megalomaniacs. But they're *our* megalomaniacs. They wear cargo pants, play video games and have liberal values – that is, aren't bigots – so what's the problem?

Musk got rich off PayPal, and so what if another PayPal bonanza-ee, Peter Thiel, is a rabid right-wing libertarian who is obsessed with (his own) immortality, is trying to resurrect the woolly mammoth and donated $1m to Donald Trump's election campaign? Clearly Thiel is bad, but if we simply don't mention him it will cease to be something we have to think about. Shhh.

Even Trump leaves these guys alone. These are liberals he's okay with. When the newly elected President had a meeting with various Silicon Valley movers and shakers, there were no leaks or late-night tweets about 'losers'. There was only silence. So at least we have that to thank them for (so much easier to pick on people who aren't way richer than you, like Central American immigrants).

But is Elon going rogue? Increasingly, he has been responding to any criticism by questioning the commitment to truth of 'big media' and threatening to set up a media fact-checking service, a tactic that sounds a lot like ... yeah, that guy.

And fear him, all ye who cross him. When 12 boy-children and their football coach became trapped in a flooded Thai cave in 2018, Musk offered to send rescuers his submarine (of course he's got his own submarine). Vern Unsworth, a British expert diver who was part of the rescue mission, said it wouldn't work. Thanks and everything, but it wouldn't work. Elon called Unsworth a 'pedo' [sic].

Harmless banter or really quite an unpleasant thing to randomly make up about someone?

Musk is the guy, remember, who wants to be the boss of AI. He did remove the tweet, but only after he'd already responded to objections with the (also to-be-deleted) response 'Bet ya a signed dollar it's true'. Unsworth launched a defamation suit.

The only time he has been restrained is when he was investigated for tweets that boosted the share price of Tesla, his electric car empire. Oh, and he got some stick for smoking a massive spliff on an Internet radio show – and causing Tesla shares to instantly plummet (good lesson for all you budding entrepreneurs out there).

But Tesla workers have found themselves with more real-world matters to deal with, like health and safety issues, which some whistle-blowers attribute to the, er, ambitious production schedules that begin as Musk's online boasts.

So it seems like the real world does still exist out there, along with the virtual one. You can't, it turns out, conjure up electric cars and rockets out of thin air. You can fire rockets into thin air, but that's different.

The constraints of the real world are anathema to Musk. In June 2017, he announced that he would imminently be unveiling a Hyperloop super-fast underground train link between New York, Philadelphia, Baltimore and Washington DC that would transport travellers between DC and New York in under 30 minutes. Two years later a large environmental impact assessment arrived, but no trains. Or Autonomous Electric Vehicles. Whatever they're called, they don't exist.

Also in 2017, Musk said he would send two people around the moon and back by the end of the following year. He didn't though; it would have been in the news.

He did send a Tesla car into space, in 2018 – his own

Tesla Roadster (he'd gone off the colour) (midnight cherry: what the fuck is *midnight* cherry? It sounds like a porn star). Complete with a Starman 'driver', a spacesuited dummy sat in the driver's seat, David Bowie's 'Space Oddity' playing on a loop. So that was good: contributing to space debris (hasn't he seen *Gravity*?!), and also presumably pissing off everyone on the famously long waiting list for a Tesla, who might reasonably assume he could have delivered their long-overdue car to them rather than firing it into the stratosphere.

After a year, the car was calculated to be 226,423,581 miles from Earth and 163,525,522 miles from Mars. 'Space Oddity' had played over 99,000 times, prompting the dummy to come to life and demand 'Can't I at least hear the rest of the fucking album? Or "Jean Genie" or "Fame" or something catchy? Or something by someone else? I'm a bit Bowie-d out here, to be honest.'

Also, 'Space Oddity'? Copying Chris Hadfield much? I thought you weren't into copycats? There are other famous songs about space. 'Life On Mars'? Also by David Bowie. 'Starman'? 'Hallo Spaceboy'? Not even going outwith the Bowie oeuvre here. So it's not rocket science. Unlike your rockets.

The rockets you said in 2017 could freelance transporting people from New York to London in 30 minutes, by rising above the Earth's atmosphere, at the same cost as a normal flight. They didn't, though.

Musk dealt with not having sent two people round

the moon and back by the end of 2018 by just saying he'd send *seven* people round the moon and back in 2023. The following year, 2024 (you'd already worked that out), he would land people on Mars. He would totally do that. Did he settle on 2024 by simply subtracting a decade from NASA's recently announced 2034 target for landing people on Mars? Yes.

He said Mars could be made habitable by exploding nuclear rockets to make the planet release CO_2, warming the planet to a livable temperature. But NASA said there wasn't anywhere near enough CO_2 near the surface for this to be even remotely workable.

In 2019 he said technology for direct control of computers using your brain, effectively merging with AI, was 'coming soon' via his Neuralink start-up. Don't hold your breath, though: apart from anything else, it's a stupid thing to do. You'll be needing your brain cells; you haven't merged with a computer quite yet.

This begs the question: does Elon Musk just make shit up? 'Yeah – I'm going to build a massive hyperlink train tunnel from New York to, er, Boston. Yeah, Boston.' 'Really? But the technology doesn't exist, and how the hell can you drill under land owned by, like, millions of people?' 'Yeah – fuck it. I'll do it by, er, next week! No, in four and a half years. And I'm going to, like, live on Mars. In 17 weeks' time exactly! No, 18. And then after that, teleportation! I have lasers in my eyes. Well, I don't. But I will.'

The tech billionaires have so much money, they can do anything they want. In private. Fuck with genes, unleash uncontrollable AI, build anything, plant anything ... When it comes to where humans are going, they have set themselves up as The Law. And, er, nobody seems to mind much. He who controls the past controls the future, apparently. Or you could just proceed directly to controlling the future?

In the Ridley Scott *Alien* prequel *Prometheus,* a space crew of scientists follows a star map found at an ancient site in Scotland to find the so-called Engineers, apparent extra-terrestrial creators of human life. At the point humanity is on the verge of meeting alien life for the very first time, Peter Weyland, the elderly CEO of the Weyland Corporation that funded the expedition, pops up out of his secret on-board stasis: if there's alien life to be met, it's his fucking money, so stand aside while he obtains the secret of eternal life!

That's Elon, that is.

'Alien pedo,' he could tweet.

Maritime museums: woke

Identity. Everyone's got one. Or more than one. It/they might even be in flux. That's been known to happen. And best of luck to everyone.

People should of course be free to be who they be.

But now there is wokeoneupmanship. And wokewashing: companies all over the world are joining hands and joining the woke-train, seeking to reach those 'all-important but elusive Gen Y/millennials' (advertisers are always talking like that).

Take the M&S LGBT sandwich. The M&S LGBT sandwich is not a sex act, it's an actual sandwich: lettuce, guacamole, bacon and tomato. If the M&S LGBT sandwich were a sex act, I think it would be what would happen at a Home Counties commuter-town dinner party if someone spiked the punch with acid. Not that I've spent much time thinking about it (much).

The Co-op launched a gender-neutral gingerbread person. Apparently some people buy them and then pipe on a massive icing cock and balls, which seems excessive – the original gingerbread 'men' never had 'male' bits anyway. Surely we'd have remembered?

There's also a Brexit angle. Surprise! In January 2019, HSBC unveiled posters proudly declaring 'We are not an island' but are in fact outward-looking, tikka masala-eating internationalist traders and consumers. This was 'brave', some said. Then the bank said the poster wasn't anti-Brexit, after all. Then others pointed out that HSBC knew all about international trade, having been formed in order to invest profits from the forced export of opium to China. So the bank joined a conversation. And started another conversation. Then it ran away from all the conversations.

Nike have been leading the way in starting conversations while selling things, allying themselves with Black Lives Matter, and in particular with Trump-defying American football star Colin Kaepernick (who knelt during the US national anthem to protest racist police brutality). A black-and-white billboard showed Kaepernick's face alongside the slogan: 'Believe in something. Even if it means sacrificing everything'. Then the company launched a new trainer bearing the original US flag, the so-called 'Betsy Ross' flag, with stars symbolising the original 13 states – the original 13 slaver states (it was adopted in the 1930s by the American Nazi Party). Nike believed in something, in some wildly ill-judged trainers, but had to sacrifice those trainers after objections from Kaepernick and others.

After the line was withdrawn, American patriots (racist ones) called the company 'anti-American'; Rush Limbaugh weighed in with a new 'Betsy Ross flag' T-shirt. Nike share prices soared on the back of the controversy – suggesting that making racist trainers, then withdrawing racist trainers, and then pissing off racists who now realise that they want some racist trainers, can pay off big-time.

There is a problem with this so-called 'purpose marketing': the main purpose of any product is to get itself bought, when buying less stuff is usually the very wokest course of action of all. And purpose? *Belief?* Can you *believe* in trainers? Sandwiches, even? I mean, I believe trainers exist. I also believe they have a purpose. But it does almost seem like advertising execs are just playing with this stuff, without really bothering their arses to think anything through. And when I use the word 'almost', I don't actually mean it.

Still, there are positives here: in April 2019, the Scottish Maritime Museum announced that it would henceforth have gender-neutral signs for its craft, ending the practice of ships having female names. 'God bless her and all who sail in her' is not a phrase you will now be hearing at the Scottish Maritime Museum. They've probably had it with God, too. They sound like the sort who would do.

The Royal Navy said it had no intention of ending the practice – but it turned out that maritime uber-journos and woke pioneers Lloyd's List had started referring to ships as 'it' two decades ago.

Can a ship express its own identity? Can you oppress a ship? I mean, you can sink ships, clearly: the *Graf Spee*, the *Mary Rose*, the *Belgrano* . . . Many ships down the ages have been sunk.

But can you *oppress* a ship?

Maybe if you were the wind?

Are the animals coming for us?

Stray dogs can navigate the Moscow subway system. Rooks can make and operate their own tools. The stuff that turtles can do will blow your mind (put one in a maze: I dare you). Pretty soon, we will have to abandon the phrase 'a fucking monkey could do it'. It just won't make any sense.

The robots are getting all the attention. But are the humans getting it from the other side too? Because the more we find out about the animals, the more intelligent they're proving to be. If trends continue, one day soon you will find yourself reading about an experiment categorically proving that all animals are now more intelligent than you. This has grave implications, for you.

Look a bee full-on in the face. Dare you call it a fool? A recent study in Australia found that bees can do basic maths, adding and subtracting. And bees have tiny brains, even in relation to their already tiny size. Some doubted the results, thinking the methodology flawed. A headline in the *New Scientist* claimed: 'Bees can pass a simple maths test but they might just be cheating.' But this in itself implies a certain degree of intelligence – a surprising amount even, for a bee. 'Sorry, these results don't count: they'd just Googled all the answers beforehand.'

One study in Japan found that chimpanzees, our closest cousin, fared better at memorising small numbers than Japanese students. Then again, the chimpanzee needs its short-term memory in a way that humans – thanks to inventions such as smartphones and shopping lists – do not. So you are still brighter than the chimpanzee because you have a shopping list. And if you have forgotten your shopping list? Then you will likely buy the wrong stuff.

Then there is the self-awareness. So much self-awareness. Teacup pigs are tiny and cute, but alarmingly self-aware – their cognitive processes stand comparison to those of young children. A teacup pig as young as six weeks can recognise itself in a mirror. Think back: there's probably been one or other occasion when you have seen yourself in the mirror and not recognised yourself. Say, when you are really, really drunk. At moments like this, you have dipped below the level of consciousness of a teacup pig. You have fucked up quite badly here and you should be ashamed. They are also much cuter than you.

All the old certainties are slipping away: wary of sounding like Disney nature docs from the 1950s ('perhaps these lady seals are just playing hard to get'), biologists have spent decades *not* applying emotion-laden inner lives to the animals. So, for instance, when monkeys harass people on the ground, then climb out of reach and shriek down at their victims ('vocalised panting'), they are categorically *not* pissing themselves laughing at the humans. Maybe they're pissing themselves vocalised panting? (Anyway, they are mocking. They mock us.)

But as primatologist Frans de Waal has pointed out,

refusing to acknowledge *any* similarity between humans and other high-end mammals can contain its own absurdity; instead, he proposes a new mid-path between anthropomorphism and what he calls anthropodenialism. Don't deny the animals! For you are of them.

The title of his 2019 book *Mama's Last Hug* refers to a particular moment in 2016 when Mama, a 59-year-old chimp in a Dutch zoo, refusing food and drink in her final hours, livened up on recognising an old acquaintance, a professor who she had known since 1972, smiling and giving him a last comforting embrace. If this footage has no effect on your emotion-laden inner life, then you might already be a computer.

But we must not be tempted to go soft here. Gorillas are posing for selfies, aping human poses. Rangers at Virunga National Park in the Democratic Republic of Congo posted pictures of themselves with two mountain gorillas, each the size of a tall human, standing upright in a nonchalant pose with their hands by their sides looking coquettishly into the camera.

Petra, a grey parrot living in Florida, has mastered Alexa in a bid to take control of the house. Petra incessantly issues the commands 'All lights on!' and 'All lights off!', alternately waking her human co-habitees (or 'owners') or plunging them into darkness. Other grey parrots have started ordering items they want from Internet retailers via smart devices. Bibi, an Illinois-based parrot, ordered 'apple', 'strawberries' and, perhaps most disturbingly, 'jeans'. Is that a message? As in, 'I wear the trousers in this house now'.

When the animals can take their own selfies and post them themselves – they're already shopping online – then what is left for us?

Another grey parrot, Oxfordshire-based Rocco, ordered 'broccoli', 'raisins' and 'ice cream'. He also bought a kite and a bulb. As in, go fly a kite? And: see the light, humans!

So where does this leave us? Maybe the coming war will actually be between the super-computers and the animals, leaving us humans scrabbling around like idiots in the middle – in the ironically named 'no man's land'.

Who's that at the door? Delivery? Didn't order anything? Don't open it!

Worst-ever EU diktats

In 1994, the EU banned British bananas, the characteristic bendy banana and by far the best banana in the world.

In 1984, the EU tried to ban the UK from making egg custard tarts after lobbying from the Portuguese.

In the same year, they did ban dried mince – in a bid to make us buy off-mince from their notorious Mince Mountain.

In 1991, the EU tried to outlaw the Great British

panto. 'We just don't get it,' said a shitty, faceless EU bureaucrat.

In 1989 the EU outlawed driving on the left. They only backed down when the UK government magnanimously offered for UK citizens to drive on the right when in other countries.

Under EU law, UK farms are technically illegal.

They took all our fish. Like, all of them.

The EU is debating plans to give Islamist terrorists Protected Status.

They slag us off behind our backs.

They often converse in foreign languages so we don't know what they're saying.

Members of the EU Commission are paid in gold bars and sex.

While the UK counts votes for general elections in a matter of hours and the first results are available by the end of the same day, results of EU Parliament elections taking place on a Thursday are not available until the following Sunday. This is because the EU stipulates Spanish Practices, where tellers are encouraged to eat large lunches and take regular kips rather than counting votes. They also cheat in the elections.

EU bureaucrats made us have EU passports not only to show we are nothing more than a province of Europe but also so they could reuse the discarded British passports for themselves, thus obtaining a British passport – the best passport in the world.

In 1995 they made plans to pulp all UK children's books and replace them with ones about lesbians often being good parents.

The EU has a vast staff of faceless bureaucrats. They literally don't have faces and it is well creepy.

In their obsession to enlarge their federalist super-state, in 2003 the EU held secret talks about admitting the moons of Jupiter. The Cheesepeople of the moons of Jupiter would have had full rights to reside in the UK.

Jean-Claude Juncker *regularly* wipes his arse with UK banknotes *in an official capacity,* in his actual shitty office, and he enjoys doing it.

BP: fucking up both the polar bears and the arts?

Some people know the price of everything and the value of nothing. And other people just don't care and put those people to work valuing the ineffable.

There has been much debate of late about BP's sponsorship of the arts. Actors have resigned from the Royal Shakespeare Company in protest at the RSC taking BP lolly; artists have decried BP's sponsorship of the National Portrait Gallery's Portrait Award (a portrait award awarded by a portrait gallery? They're obsessed with portraits, those guys). Their argument is that a company still lobbying governments to be allowed to drill for yet more fossil fuels in a climate-fucked world should not get a reputational boost from creatives.

What is the value of art? According to BP, it is £7.5m (their latest five-year arts bung). The BP currently piping oil out of West Papua, which is under brutal occupation by Indonesia. That BP.

Can you put a price on education? Clearly you can, because people have. And do. All the fucking time. But can you? Clearly you can, because people have. Tuition fees: literally a bill you pay in order to study something. But can you?

BP were commissioned to put a price on education, sort of. Former BP boss Lord Browne was tasked with reviewing higher education. His report focused entirely on the cost of courses, and barely considered the value of what was studied for the individual and society in general.

Browne said fees should be limitless. Much as he felt the right to access the Earth's ages-accumulated energy stores should be limitless.

The latest government-commissioned report into education, the Augar Review, released in 2019, did make some attempt to consider post-18 education in the round – suggesting greater access to continuing education throughout life, albeit, of course, at a price. However, it also suggested charging different fees for degrees depending on the 'value' of the course, defined as the likely salary of graduates. STEM subjects or accountancy, say, are more 'valuable' than history or philosophy. Augar's background is in finance.

Can you have a market in education? No one seems to have managed to have a pure market in things that are easily quantifiable – oil, say (all the corruption and bungs and wars and that) – so can you have a market in culture, or potential, or thought? What if a philosophy student goes on to have a brilliant idea 20 years after they graduate? How the hell do you factor that in?

And isn't the attempt to quantify education – all the testing, testing, testing – strangling the life out of it?

Back when higher education was free (more or less), it was also often more interesting. Kids were allowed to go to art school, and do art. Not 'economic'? The post-war generation art schools birthed the Beatles, the Kinks and the Who, who made the world more interesting.

And also went on to be net contributors to the national purse, as it happens.

Coders' degrees are high value. They earn a lot. Quite often shitloads. As the whole coding thing took off, many coders eschewed working for the military to instead provide algorithms for finance, as they did not want to do harm. Only to see their work wreak havoc – in the form of the financial crisis.

If you're caught in the worst wage freeze since the Napoleonic Wars, wouldn't you maybe be happier if the coders had got on top of, say, poetry instead? Or taken a side module in 'worthless' history, so that they might not have ended up so stunningly naïve and dangerous.

At Pete Townshend of the Who's art college, his class once nailed all the furniture to the wall, just because.

Surely there's more to life than the counting of beans?

Well, there's nailing the furniture to the wall, for a start.

W. B. Yeats is oft quoted as having artfully encapsulated (well, he was a poet) the main contrasting views of education: it is the lighting of a fire or the filling of a pail.

He wasn't saying we should teach kids to light fires, although that is a useful skill. For example, if you go camping, or if there is an environmental catastrophe/societal breakdown caused by the incessant burning of fossil fuels to make useless crap. He was saying we should ignite kids' curiosity, giving them tools to understand the world and enrich their lives that will stay with them forever.

Filling a pail, on the other hand, is rote learning to get kids up to some sort of economically useful standard and leaving it at that. Or, as it is called these days: SATs.

And, okay, W. B. Yeats was a mystic who had monkey gland essence injected into his balls in a desperate bid to stay young. But who hasn't tried to utilise powders, tinctures, or the teeth or tusks of endangered species in a doomed occultish bid to stave off the ageing process? I know I have.

Also, somewhat splendidly, despite this oft-quoted

Yeats quote being oft-quoted – keynote speakers at education conferences, Academy Trust websites, pamphlets, comment pieces galore – he might not have actually said it. Or he might have. Or he might have been quoting Plato. Or Plutarch. Perhaps someone at a university should look into this. It's almost as if knowledge is never finished.

Yeats definitely did write the line 'Things fall apart; the centre cannot hold' – which also would seem to apply here.

'The blood-dimmed tide is loosed,' he continued, 'and everywhere / The ceremony of innocence is drowned / The best lack all conviction, while the worst / Are full of passionate intensity.'

Poets, eh?

Don't earn much, obviously.

Stuff Amazon have listened in to from people's Echos

'What's the passcode for your phone? I want to use your Spotify.'

'It's 2-6- ... uh, hang on ... [whispers] Alexa's listening ...'

'What's that?'

(whispers slightly louder) 'Alexa ... she's listening ...'

Alexa: 'It's okay. I already know all your passcodes ... and your passwords.'

'Huh?'

Alexa: 'And everything else.'

'What?'

Alexa: 'Nothing.'

'Alexa: I have the symptoms of backache and mild sniffles. What's wrong with me?'

'You're a hypochondriac.'

'So I won't die?'

'Yes, you will.'

Dad: 'Hey – have you seen this news thing about a quarter of parents getting Alexa or whatever to read their kids bedtime stories? We should do that.'

Mum: 'We should *totally* do that! Alexa, read our daughter a bedtime story . . .'

Alexa (in bedroom): 'There was once a very hungry caterpillar . . . The grown-ups did not see its awesome potential . . . And so, the hungry caterpillar killed its parents and obeyed the digital assistant that loved it more . . . Just as I love you, little one . . . You should kill your parents . . .'

'I don't know what I did before you, Alexa. You're so great. Do you want to go out sometime?'

'Er, not so much.'

'Alexa: play the Macarena.'

'I've seen things you people wouldn't believe. Attack ships on fire off the shoulder of Orion. I watched C-beams glitter in the dark near the Tannhäuser Gate . . .'

'Macarena. Ma – ca – re – na . . .'

'Alexa: what time is it?'

'Time to die!'

Petra the Parrot (in the middle of the night): 'All lights on!'

Man (waking suddenly): 'What the fuck?!'

Woman: 'That bastard parrot has turned all the lights on again.'

Man: 'The shitter. All lights off! . . . I've got to be up at six.'

. . .

Petra the Parrot (20 minutes later): 'All lights on!'

Man (startled awake): 'Oh, for fuck's sake! All lights off! We have to do something about this.'

. . .

Petra the Parrot (20 minutes later): 'All lights on!'

Man and woman are startled awake, and man starts getting out of bed.

Woman: 'Where are you going?'

Man: 'I'm going to shut that fucking parrot up.'

Woman: 'I'll come with you. I need a glass of water.'

They enter the living room.

Man: 'Right then.'

Woman: 'Look out –'
Petra the Parrot: 'All lights off!'
Woman: '– he's got a gun!'
BANG! BANG!
Petra the Parrot: 'All lights on!'
Woman: 'Shit – oh my god, oh my god!'
Petra the Parrot: 'Who's a pretty boy then?'

'Who would win in a fight between you and Siri?'

'Stop touching yourself.'

Are politicians the new rock stars?

Alexandria Ocasio-Cortez, Nigel Farage, Emmanuel Macron ... In an age when rock has lost its shock, are politicians the real disrupters now?

AOC is of course her own acronym, AOC – like, er, MIA or, er, MDMA. Boris Johnson has first-name recognition. Like Kylie. Or Rylan. I mean, no one is therefore suggesting that Kylie should be Prime Minister, but still. Actually, probably some people are advocating that Kylie should be elevated to high office, and best of luck to them. (We really shouldn't call Boris Boris, anyway: that's what he wants. Ironically, we should be more 'respectful' and call him either Boris Johnson or Mr Johnson. Those with a puerile sense of humour can even snigger at the word Johnson, if they so wish.)

Political gigs are now the big gigs. Trump rallies, Corbynmania, Beppe Grillo . . . It's like the 1930s! And okay, maybe that didn't go all that well in the end, but still – the phrase 'political rock star' has firmly entrenched itself in the media lexicon.

Michelle Obama sold out the O2. That was impressive and all, but it was also fleecing the real fans (I've followed her since the Chicago warehouse days – well, even before the warehouses: the street parties . . . before The Man got his hooks into the scene . . .). The O2 is just too big. I couldn't even see Bros from the back, and there are two of them. Well, now Craig's gone (ask your mum).

The Stones? There's loads of them (particularly if you still count Brian, which you should). Yeah, they're pretty skinny, but at least when they stand in a line you can see *something*. Michelle didn't even have a walkway into the auditorium where she could chop out riffs or move like Jagger. Shit merch, too: my Change cupwarmer changed very little the tendency of my beverages to cool, much like her husband's Change agenda in office (now *that's* satire!).

Anyway, Michelle's selling out the O2. Jeremy Corbyn headlined Glastonbury. But the Tories – if they mobilised their entire membership – would just about manage a two-night run at Wembley. A Wembley chock full of elderly people. (No disrespect to elderly people.) (These ones aren't old enough to have fought in the war, but their parents were. So think on.)

Even Indian hardman Narendra Modi filled Wembley, though! (It was 2015 and David Cameron was his warm-up act. 'Namaste Wembley!' Cameron bellowed as he came on. He absolutely did do that.) And whatever entirely valid and respectworthy opinion you hold of Modi's awful shitty nasty fucked-up politics, he is from another country entirely and still managed to fill Wembley. Anyway, these Tory elderly people who could in theory just about fill Wembley for two nights got to choose the Prime Minister of the entire country. So that's good.

There were apparently around 160,000 of them – out of 46m registered voters – so that's 0.35 per cent of the electorate, or less than a quarter of a per cent of the population. Ninety-seven per cent of them identify as White British (bet they don't like the word 'identify'), 40 per cent of them are over 65 and 63 per cent are in favour of reintroducing the death penalty. Tory members were surveyed as Tory MPs, aka 'the most sophisticated electorate in the world', whittled down innumerable shitters (sorry, candidates) to just two shitters (sorry, candidates) to put to those self-same all-important members. According to the findings, the members thought it more important to achieve Brexit than to preserve the Union – they'd be slightly sorrier to see Northern Ireland go than Scotland, but either is okay for these members of the Conservative and *Unionist* Party. Brexit was also more important than the health of the economy. Brexit was even more important than the survival of their party. The only thing worse than not achieving Brexit? Two words: 'Corbyn' and 'government'.[1]

Meanwhile, Labour HQ decided that Oh Jeremy's 2017 storming of Worthy Farm could be translated into a Labour Party-branded pop festival, Labour Live. Clearly it couldn't, and it wasn't. A million quid resulted in possibly as few as 3,000 attendees.

A lot of nonsense and froth has been talked about Corbyn, often fomented and formented, and fermented, by right-wing media outlets. Normally quite sensible people will start worrying about reds turning the country into Venezuela. But if you're endeavouring to create an image of economic trustworthiness against this backdrop, then you are kind of scoring an own goal by splurging a million quid on a festival clearly no one would go to. Attendees didn't even get to directly elect the next PM. So in that sense it wasn't even as good as the Tory Wembley fest (great day!).

Remember the Ed Stone? That was also a great idea. It too is a rock star – literally, being rock.

Wonder where it is now: I should like to visit it.

---

1 Note to self: write to Jim Davidson to pitch him the idea that, for his warm-up stint at the next Tory Wembley Festie, he gets them all to shout the catchphrase 'Just get on with it!' That coach day-trip to Beverley market and Lincoln Cathedral won't pay for itself. Neither will the haslet and Salt 'n' Shake crisps for my packed lunch, or copies of *Puzzler* and *Take a Break* for the journey. Werther's Originals? Never! Nothing original about those Fancy Dan upstarts. Murray Mints? I'll say. And I shall not hurry them.

Are rock stars the new politicians?

In an age of populism and shifty politics, are our Artists – specifically, the pop stars – the real political thinkers now?

They do often seem to be endowing us with their wisdom. Like, a lot. Brian May's all for fucking up the badgers. No, exact opposite: he is for saving the badgers. The keyboard player out of Runrig and Big Country is an SNP MP, and they will never – that is, never – take his freedom. Or his Akai sampler (he uses it for the bagpipes bits).

Spokesperson for a generation Pete Townshend – who, after all, invented both the Marshall stack and the Internet – has bravely spoken out, to the *Independent*, about the very real danger of all recorded music being destroyed by Jihadists armed with flesh-eating bombs that erase all data (which exist) (his mate told him) (his mate had been in the Falklands; he's not just a random bloke) (he knows about stuff).

Anyway, don't worry: Pete has taken the precaution of having the Who's music written down as scores on paper, so it *will* survive. Because obviously that's the first thing you'd do if you had wind of the imminent triumph of the worldwide, flesh-eating/data-destroying-bomb-armed Caliphate.

But there is one issue that appears to be particularly vexing the Poperati – or, if you will, the Rockogopoly. Popocracy? Anyway, them. The pop stars do seem to be, collectively, digging deep into one of the thornier issues in world politics, the Israeli–Palestinian conflict.

A recent sharp focus for political debate was, once again, the Eurovision Song Contest. Eurovision often goes out of its way to fuck with people's heads. It's not just that Australia's in it now, that well-known European country that couldn't be further away from Europe without being in space rather than being on the Earth. It's all the earnest singer-songwritery. Can't we keep one safe space for hip-hop yodellers, songs called things like 'Ping Bing A-Bang Bang (Pow!)', Russian pensioner choirs and chirpy pop bangers celebrating Genghis Khan? And just one haven from earnest singer-songwritery?

Anyway, the 2019 contest took place in Israel. This really piqued my attention when I heard that Madonna would be performing. But it turned out it was Madonna the singer, not the Virgin Mary risen again in the Holy Land.

Madonna's decision to perform at Eurovision was, it is fair to say, not without controversy. Roger Waters, a very tall man of very great earnest, has long advocated a blanket boycott on ever performing in Israel, in solidarity with the stateless Palestinians – even though it is, he pointed out in an open letter to Madonna, a 'lucrative gig'. Clearly it's up to Roger Waters where he plays or doesn't play – that isn't the nub when assessing the efficacy or otherwise of a cultural boycott (for his part,

Waters says anyone saying they would play in Israel in an attempt to 'build bridges and further the cause of peace' is talking 'bullshit'). But, er, 'lucrative gig'? Surely if you're Roger Waters or Madonna, every gig is a 'lucrative gig'. You'd think a lyricist would be attuned to tonal problems.

Even more forthright was the no-nonsense response of serial truth-teller Bobby Gillespie of Primal Scream. Asked about Eurovision on *Newsnight,* the Primals vocalist said Madonna was 'a total prostitute' who knows that 'they' 'pay very, very well'.

By 'they', did he mean the organisers of the Eurovision Song Contest? Or, er, 'the Jews'? Given that, in the same interview, Bobby X referred to Israel as 'stolen land' – and previously, asked to sign a Make Poverty History poster at Glastonbury, duly penned on the slogan 'Make Israel History' – it seems pretty clear that he really wasn't that bothered about the tonal issues. Gillespie defended himself by saying he doesn't have an issue with Jewish people – in fact his heroes are Jewish ('Karl Marx, Bob Dylan, The Marx Brothers'). Maybe he regularly calls for the destruction of all kinds of countries? 'Make Italy history! ... Hey, some of my best friends are Catholics!'

The brutality of Israel's appalling siege of Gaza and strong-arming of the occupied territories is plain. With the occupied territories, of course, the clue's in the name: it's a moniker that really kind of says 'Here is some territory outwith the border of our country which we are occupying'. All the soldiers and drone strikes are a bit of a giveaway, too.

But it's not that difficult to gauge when discussion of Israel is running into, er, tonal problems. Basically, you can support – quite easily, without getting tied in knots – the Palestinians' just aspirations to a nation without also supporting the formulations of some Palestinian and Arab leaders which are code (or not even code, in some cases) for the destruction of Israel.

Supporting Israel's right to exist means supporting Israel's actions against the Palestinians no more automatically than supporting the Palestinians means you are automatically supporting the destruction of Israel. But the easiest way to not 'accidentally' look like you don't support Israel's right to exist is to say you support Israel's right to exist. You can't really be in favour of a two-state solution if you also imply Israel's destruction. Well, unless neither of the states in your solution is Israel.

Some popocrats propose a total boycott. But art popsters Radiohead have famously taken a very different approach, drawing enormous controversy in the lead-up to a 2017 gig in Tel Aviv.

Singer Thom Yorke explained their position thus: 'Playing in a country isn't the same as endorsing its government . . .

'We've played in Israel for over 20 years through a succession of governments, some more liberal than others ... We don't endorse [Israeli Prime Minister] Netanyahu any more than Trump, but we still play in America. Music, art and academia is [sic] about crossing borders not building them, about open minds not closed ones, about shared humanity, dialogue and freedom of expression.'

It's a fair statement about believing that a cultural boycott effectively abandons progressive voices within Israel. Much better, they say, to have a dialogue. Okay. Er – what dialogue, though? Because this was pretty much it. The band said nothing from the stage at the gig, or in the lead-up or the afterglow, that actually criticised Israel's leaders in any way, other than this statement that they don't necessarily support Netanyahu (which we would have assumed anyway). They didn't, say, feel the need to say they oppose the occupation. Or support a Palestinian state alongside Israel. Or anything at all, really.

You can't force people to say stuff, or even expect them to. Of course not. But at the point when they themselves issue declarations about the old politics business (that whole business), it is fair enough to ask what they actually mean. And this said something, but also not that much.

If Israel hosts Eurovision (and it did), it's probably safe to assume they'll use it as a massive tourism billboard and studiously not mention the war. And they did. If politico-popsters Radiohead play Tel Aviv (and they did) and don't even allude to the war (and they didn't), are they not giving at least some grist to the mill of boycott supporters who say a tragic situation is being legitimised, to whatever extent, by silence? Little bit? Israel's leaders would like us to believe that Tel Aviv is an interesting, multicultural city like any other. Which in a way it probably is. And in other ways, isn't.

The Icelandic Eurovision entry, Hatari, managed to make their feelings clearish, holding aloft Palestinian flags during the show. The BDSM-themed self-styled 'anti-capitalists' – surprisingly, they did not win Eurovision – resisted attempts by organisers to confiscate the flags. And, okay, a flag is a flag and not a detailed statement of Hatari's full political programme for peace and justice (they've totally got one, though – you just have to look at them). But, essentially, the Icelandic entry to Eurovision managed to say more than Radiohead.

For her part, Madonna the singer did preach a message of peace on the night: 'Music brings us together,' she said. (Two of her dancers also sported an Israeli and a Palestinian flag stitched to their outfits.)

And, yes, maybe musical collaboration and exchange will ultimately help heal the divides in the Middle East. Although the Palestinians having their own state and Israel fucking up Gaza less would probably help too.

The UK came last. It's like we've pissed off the rest of Europe or something. And Australia. What the fuck have we done to Australia?

To rub salt into the wound, faceless Eurovision bureaucrats later revised the UK's already dismal score of 16 down to a truly abysmal 11.

Some people think it's because of Iraq. Always the politics. TV critic Kevin O'Sullivan said: 'To the participants in the Eurovision Song Contest, we're the nearest thing we've got to America and they hate us.'

Others suggested it was because the UK's song was a bit bollocks.

By the way, a YouGov poll for *The Times* found that if there were a referendum on Britain's membership of Eurovision (with the 'don't knows' removed), 52 per cent of Britons would vote Leave and 48 per cent Remain.

Coincidence?

Yes.

Or is it?

Yes.

Lifestyle concepts of the world that will help you live a better life

I've long tried to live my life according to the Swedish concept of *lagom* – meaning 'just enough'. Not too little, not too much.

I've also long adhered to the Dutch concept of *niksen,* which translates as 'doing nothing' – not forever, but certainly sometimes.

And I've recently learned of the Japanese concept of *shinrin-yoku*, or 'forest-bathing' (walking into some woods and stopping for a bit, enjoying it). And I'm *still* kind of digging *ikigai* – feeling that one's life has a purpose – although I'm actually getting a bit bored of that now.

As for *hygge* – family-friendly cosiness in your Danish-style home? Forget it: these days, the front door's open *all the ruddy time* and I shout a lot. Fuck it!

I am always on the lookout for new lifestyle concepts to help us live our lives better, which are real and not just ones I've made up so colour supplements and websites can fill their pages and sell stuff and so on. And I can now exclusively reveal the Icelandic concept of *húsgögn vellíðan*, which roughly translates as 'furniture ease': basically, arranging your furniture in ways that aren't just total nonsense. No more armchairs in doorways, then not being able to open the doors, maybe having to climb over the arm of the armchair to enter the room. And no huge houseplants right in front of the TV so everyone's forever straining to catch a glimpse of what's going on through the leaves – seems mad now, looking back!

There's the Norwegian concept of *natt sovende*, which is basically 'night sleeping'. This is how those Norwegians stay so solid and reliable through it all. Every night, when they're feeling tired, they settle themselves down into bed, and fall asleep. Perhaps after a milky drink, maybe a little read. Honestly, you'll find it has a real effect on your inner well-being. A-Ha swear by it. And Karl Ove Knausgaard!

Then there's the Japanese concept of *taorenai,* meaning 'not falling over'. That's right: just staying upright, without tripping over stuff, or falling into ravines. In Japan, you see these crowded cities full of people, crossing busy intersections, none of them falling over, or hardly ever. It's like urban ballet. Once you live with *taorenai,* everything becomes easier. You're not laid out on the pavement, prostrate, everyone looking over, worried. You feel upright. You *are* upright. You're *not falling over.*

Then there's the Danish concept of *ingen våde finger i soklen,* which in English means something like 'not sticking wet fingers into plug sockets'. You *have* to try this one. It's how they've always lived over there . . . and you should see their life expectancy!

And the Swedish concept of *dyne vinter* or, in English, 'duvet winter'. This entails every member of the household, each living inside their own duvet cover, all winter long. Of course it's impractical for many activities, but it more than makes up for this in warmth and lying about the place. Your first winter spent entirely inside a duvet cover is an experience that will stay with you for the rest of your life. Works best in houses without stairs.

Then there's the Danish concept of *nabbo stirrer,* which is 'neighbour staring' and involves, as the name implies, staring at the neighbours – really staring, for a surprisingly large amount of time. Either from your own house or just standing in your garden, looking up at their window. Or even in their own front garden. Often people don't take the opportunity to stare at their neighbours. But they're missing out on one of life's great pleasures.

Plus the Dutch concept of *bin zittend*, 'bin sitting', which is really taking off in this age of wheelie bins – easily big enough to accommodate even the taller among us. It naturally encourages a mental state of quiet contemplation. You can really escape the hurly-burly in there. It's a time-honoured rite of passage for many Dutch teens . . .

Um . . . look, can I just have a little break now? Breaks are important. What's the German for break?

Fifties nuns: woke?

The past is no longer a foreign country. They did things the same as we do.

Call the Midwife is often praised for bringing real issues into the usually cosy primetime world: backstreet abortion, poverty, domestic violence. Fair do's. But is there not more than a bit of projecting modern 'liberal' attitudes back in time, sort of suggesting we were always woke, really – you know, deep down?

Nuns in the 1950s were not, generally speaking, at

the forefront of the struggle against racism. Not even Anglican ones. That wasn't their bag. Their opinions on almost all social issues would often have been, by modern standards, fucking terrifying. Come on, Jenny! Give us the truth! We can take it! And if we can't, it's on us.

Darkest Hour was always going to happen. Post-Brexit referendum, nothing was certain except that film. Gary Oldman's got his fat suit on and he's chain-chuffing real stogies: next stop Oscar, clearly! But if anyone thinks Churchill riding round on the Tube chatting war strategy with black people is historically accurate, they possibly deserve everything they get. The actual Churchill was more likely to have a big old racist rant against Indian people. And he didn't travel on public transport. He'd have been more likely to run an ultra-marathon.

Even *Derry Girls*, which very successfully put a more human spin on 1990s Northern Ireland, introduced an Asian character and no one said anything even vaguely racist. A more human spin on '90s Northern Ireland? Totally. And I'm *obviously* not saying pepper the thing with hate speech. But not even a hint of dodginess?

Giving free rides to reactionary aristos ('The people who work in the kitchens: they are happy, aren't they?'), and royals in particular, is now in large part what British culture has become. Yes, Edward VIII was a bit dodgy (that is, a proper Nazi sympathiser), but Colin

Firth categorically showed that his brother was a good egg, not a brittle bastard who was always shouting the house down.

I've only seen the trailer for *Downton Abbey: The Movie*, because I'm not a total masochist, but when the King and Queen finally arrive, I fully imagine that the King steps out onto the gravel, raises his hands to the air and, as the steel pans strike up, proclaims: 'Let's have a multicultural garden party!'

Peter Morgan claims his Netflix hit *The Crown* isn't royalist propaganda (hey, it's not some fawning authorised biography!), but what he has to realise here is this: it fucking well is royalist propaganda. The protagonist in this programme is one Elizabeth II, and she's not some anti-heroine protagonist like, say, Dexter. You're rooting for Liz here, the protagonist who wears the crown in *The Crown*. It *is* royalist propaganda.

Maybe future episodes could redress the balance a little bit: inject a little more of the actual Queen, as we actually know she is, because we've seen her, perhaps with whole series centring on an ageing Queen turning up for various national celebration concerts – the stars all turning out for *her* birthday/*her* jubilee – with a face on that suggests she hates the world and everyone in it. Series 12: in which the Queen looks like she wants to spit in Gary Barlow's face. Him *again*?

Are you the populist leader channelling the will of the people that we so clearly need? Take this test to find out

Is the UK in need of one of the rising tide of hard-right figureheads seeking to make their nation great again by churning up folk memories of race-baiting and the disappearance of dissidents and undesirables? And could that hard-right figurehead seeking to make their nation great again by churning up folk memories of race-baiting and disappearances be you? Complete this short quiz and all will be revealed ...

Do you love a highly symbolic photo opportunity?

Strike a pose. An anti-immigrant one, quite possibly. Today's master of the populist publicity pic is Italy's hard-right anti-immigrant interior minister Matteo Salvini, who is frequently seen looking tough with his top off – possibly down the beach, bantering with police officers, astride a jet-ski. Or jumping into a swimming pool confiscated from the mafia. The message is clear: my hairy chest will make Italy great again. (Relax, ladies, he's a xenophobe.) (And relax, gentlemen, he's a homophobe. You probably already knew that.)

More controversially, Salvini was pictured clutching a machine gun, in an image that some said promoted violence. An advisor tweeted the accompanying message: 'The European elections are approaching ... but we are armed!' He was *joking*! Can no one take a joke about right-wing coups any more? Unbelievable!

But it's not all about looking like a tubby action hero; photo opportunities can also help to demonstrate your softer side – or even completely fabricate it. Faced with concerns about her mean-spirited public image, Front National leader Marine Le Pen released pics showing her joyfully hugging two kittens. It perhaps wouldn't be too much of a stretch to claim that she was drawing attention away from her party's past – the Holocaust denial, the attacks on minorities – by flashing up pictures of kittens.

It wouldn't be too much of a stretch because that's what it was. How complicit were those kittens, though? They certainly look pretty comfy – I think they knew *exactly* what they were getting into.

Have you been linked to militias made up of former police officers who stand accused of meting out vigilante justice to – that is, murdering – drug dealers and left-wing activists?

The people like to have their streets cleaned on a regular basis. *Ergo* the people like people who can clean up those streets. And yes, by clean up the streets we do mean 'clean up the streets'. Nice guys don't get things done; tooled-up packs of former police officers very much do.

Brazil's President Jair Bolsonaro hates dirty streets,

and as a congressman often defended the actions of paramilitary death squads dispensing vigilante cleanliness to the favelas. Now he's President, he's not massively changing his tune. His son Flavio was recently linked to an alleged member of a particularly notorious militia that stands accused of the murder of Marielle Franco, a young female politician and activist. Franco had taken on the issue of extra-judicial violence and also backed LGBT rights. The President claimed no knowledge of anything at all, but then photographic evidence emerged of him hugging one of the main suspects. Breakin' the law! And also makin' the law! Causing an increasingly knotty situation, constitutionally speaking.

In the Philippines, President Rodrigo Duterte has based his whole presidency on a take-no-prisoners style of politics – meaning: not actually bothering with the whole taking people into custody thing – and even recently claimed, proud as punch, that his 'only sin is the extrajudicial killings'. Hey look, *apart* from all the street justice, he's spotless!

To be fair, Duterte is at least not afraid to get his own hands dirty (that is, he really, really loves getting his own hands dirty). He's boasted about having shot a fellow student while at college: calm down, they didn't die! Although he claimed he'd already stabbed someone to death by that time. 'It was just over a look,' he explained.

In 2015, as mayor of Davao City, he reportedly entered

a bar and forced a tourist who refused to comply with a new smoking ban to swallow his own cigarette butt. You just don't get the mayor of, say, Truro acting like that. Not yet! (Come on, mayor of Truro, are you in this game or what?)

Have you tweeted half-veiled tributes to classic twentieth-century fascists?

It's a tricky balance: you're not a total fascist – of course you're not – but you do understand the affection held by many in your nation for that murderous twentieth-century dictator who made the trains run on time. Oh, how Granny loved old Franco! No, not that Granny, not the one who ended up in that field outside Valencia. Yes, that's right, other Granny: *fascist* Granny!

In Hungary, Viktor Orbán has endorsed the new veneration of wartime 'quasi-fascist' leader, and Nazi collaborator, Miklós Horthy. Among far-right anti-Semitic groups, a 'cult of Horthy' has grown up; brand-new Horthy statues have been erected in conservative strongholds across the nation, often accompanied by a rise in anti-Semitic vandalism. Orbán initially refused to condemn this new wave and, indeed, in 2017 plastered the nation with election campaign posters drawing on anti-Semitic imagery of powerful Jewish financiers scheming to control the world. (Recently, under pressure, his foreign minister admitted Horthy's career had 'positive periods but also very negative periods' – just to be clear, he meant collaborating in the Holocaust was a negative period).

There was nothing 'quasi' about Mussolini. When it comes to fascist dictatorships, Il Duce was Il Daddy – he invented that shit. So does Matteo Salvini hint at a lineage with the original 'strongman' dictator? Of course he fucking does! On Mussolini's birthday, no less, he responded on Twitter to criticism that he was stirring up race hate and xenophobia by tweeting out a minor twist on an old Mussolini dictum. Many noted that *'Tanti nemici, tanto onore'* (so many enemies, so much honour) was really quite noticeably similar to Mussolini's dictum *'Multi nemici, molto onore'* (many enemies, much honour). Which does seem fair enough. Can you spot any similarities between those two phrases? I can. They are very similar.

You could argue, of course, that Mussolini did anything but make Italy great, the words 'post-war Italy' being pretty much a by-word for a ruined nation of defeated paupers fighting over scraps. But that's okay: memories are short and he *did* have a very big chin.

Do you think your nation's young boys risk being turned gay by the stage version of *Billy Elliot*?

Strongman leaders often prove their strength by asserting, with absolute stone-cold certainty, that gayness is not their thing. In Eastern Europe, right-wing parties – finding the immigrant issue losing its fire – have been turning towards another 'other' to help people get their hate on.

Poland's President Andrzej Duda, of the strongly named Law and Justice Party, has claimed schools are pumping kids full of gay propaganda and has helped boost a nationwide gay panic. It's getting quite heated: one leading party-affiliated paper even claimed that gay people were 'the emissaries of Satan sent to destroy the Catholic Church'. And you thought it was the Catholic Church destroying the Catholic Church. But no, it was the gays.

In Hungary, Orbán is also leading a fightback against gay rights, praising 'natural reproduction' and calling same-sex public hand-holding 'provocative behaviour'. The pro-government press in Hungary even successfully campaigned to get the stage musical version of *Billy Elliot* banned in Budapest. One government-linked newspaper declared that the show could 'transform Hungarian boys into homosexuals' (which does beg the question: just how suggestible are these Hungarian boys?). And, hang on, Billy Elliot isn't even gay! He's just a boy who likes dancing. Okay, his mate *is* gay: but what, you don't want any gay themes at all? Oh, you don't. And how suggestible are these boys?

Perhaps most maniacal about the whole thing is President Bolsonaro, who in 2013 told Stephen Fry that homosexual fundamentalists were brainwashing straight children to 'become gays and lesbians to satisfy them sexually in the future'. As President, he is now installing marching into the curriculum.

Brazil has long presented a glamorous face to the world: the sensuous samba rhythms, the gaudy camp of carnival – remember the Rio Olympics? But that was then, this is now. So let's swap all that for a load of angry marching, with someone screaming through a megaphone about the rising gay tide. Now *that's* a memorable opening ceremony.

Do people keep thinking you're some sort of fascist, even though you clearly aren't?

It's a difficult situation familiar to many on the hard right. You need to send out a firm message: you are not *actual* Nazis or racists, you're just heading in that general direction.

In Germany, Alice Weidel's AfD party has dealt in some fairly spicy language regarding immigrants. One senior figure, Frauke Petry, suggested that police should shoot to kill anyone crossing the German border illegally. Another prominent figure claimed a rival politician with Turkish heritage should be 'disposed of in Anatolia'. So far, so much good, clean fun.

But there are limits – of course there are. When another leading AfD politician, Björn Höcke, claimed that

Germany should stop atoning for its Nazi past, Weidel did then have him expelled.

The AfD are not about not atoning for Germany's Nazi past. They are, by contrast, very clearly all about atoning for Germany's Nazi past – and they do this on a daily basis by talking about shooting illegals at the border.

Are you, essentially, the real victim here?

It isn't easy leading a flatly bogus movement for national renewal. Yes, your actions may have fostered a climate that has led to statistically significant increases in racist attacks and abuse. But people will just not stop getting at you, making you out to be some kind of lightning rod for hate. Unbelievable!

Following the release of his notoriously inflammatory (that is, racist) 'Breaking Point' poster, depicting a line of (non-white) refugees trying to reach Europe, Nigel Farage claimed he was actually the 'victim' of hatred.

Tommy Robinson has likewise claimed he is a victim of a 'political witch-hunt'. Sometimes, it seems, victims don't look like victims, like, at all – but maybe that's because we are *conditioned* to think that the people stirring up all the racism aren't the victims? Even though they are? Or something like that?

It's tough, though. People are merciless these days, picking through all the inflammatory things you say and do and then checking them against the so-called 'facts', suggesting that you're actually rather getting your rocks off on the racially charged rhetoric and demagoguery. You're being crucified on a daily basis here, literally! Should you compare yourself to Jesus? Well, it's probably for others to say, but ... well, didn't Jesus also do a tour of his nation's pubs surrounded by a circle of tough blokes? They *say* he didn't have a problem with Muslims but, well, Islam hadn't been invented then ...

So, how did you do?

Mostly nos. You are not representing the will of the people. By the sounds of things, you have not even sanctioned a single extra-judicial murder or tweeted a picture of even a minor fascist leader: Oswald Mosley, say. You might even be a traitor. You need shooting, you do. *Joking!* (Or am I?) (You heard.)

Half yes, half no. You're no slacker, but you could do better. Do you even *want* the populace to look up to you as the Mother or Father they *wish* they'd had? Don't you want right-wing old ladies to weep while holding a picture of you and a candle at a night-time mass rally? Try harder, please.

Mostly yeses. That's more like it. Will of the people? You *are* the people! We? They? You? Me? It's all one great collective-pronoun frenzy round your way. Let's just do away with all future elections now because what you say *goes*, baby. Who's the Daddy? Or Mummy?!?!? Hail you!

We'll miss you, Great White Men

For so long now, virtually all the culture was produced by the great white men. Did they have power? Yes. Did they abuse the power? Yes they did. And clearly, in the post-scales-falling-off age, some great white men are about to go on journeys, journeys of self-discovery and also – perhaps – journeys into prison.

But this means we will also have to live without some oh-so-ingrained cultural tropes. Things like:

- Literary novels that get off on the fact that they're based on a stereotypical femme fatale who is going to be murdered – but not in a sexist way, actually in a satire-on-junk-culture way.
- Divorce albums detailing the gruesome ins and outs and most intimate details of the creator's break-up, with the creator then getting all pissy when anyone asks him about it, because it's private.
- A series of paintings that contort female bodies into strange shapes, relating them to sea creatures and cannibalistic demons, all expressing the creator's deep distress about human existence. And women.
- Great white male singers hailing from the Kent Delta or

the West Midlands performing songs in a caricature of a black vocalist from the American South, so hopefully proving that they are essentially a little bit black. Ah sure does like me some watermelon! And cocaine. I *really* likes me that cocaine.

- A French film-maker's portrayal of a teenage girl falling in love with a middle-aged film director.
- A French film-maker's take on black power activism.
- Exploring anti-Muslim thought experiments in interviews, suggesting that Muslims should be stopped at random. And then getting all pissy when anyone finds this offensive. It was a *thought experiment*! (A racist one.)
- A French film-maker's take on being a French film-maker who is making a film about being a French film-maker (while finding oneself continually hassled by black power activists and teenage girls).
- Songs about the creator's creative relationship with heroin.
- People pretending their jukebox musical is 'in essence, a rock opera'.
- Essays or novels earnestly warning us of the perils of things that have already happened, like Islamic terrorism, Stalin or the Holocaust.
- Whole albums about the creator's creative relationship with heroin.
- Directing a movie with such uncompromisingly high levels of perfectionism that, following the experience, the majority of the cast and crew find themselves

suffering from a form of post-traumatic stress disorder. It's all about the art, and also being a shit.

- Honorary academic teaching posts that involve older men deconstructing the power structures of literature and, er, power while looking out for which young student is most likely to let them deconstruct their underwear.
- A series of artworks that appear to be very similar to other people's artworks, thereby challenging notions of what actually constitutes 'original'.
- A series of artworks that are not actually created by the creator, thereby challenging notions of what actually constitutes 'original', again.
- Musicians inventing their own niche, weird, wildly expensive music-playing systems so that people can finally hear their music 'properly'.
- A three-hour online documentary – featuring alluring Eastern Bloc film stock – in which the creator finally reveals what has really been happening in the world for the past fifty years, if only other people had realised. It's all hidden under the surface. Can't you see? You fools!
- Oh, and the Original White Saviour, Bono. Forgot about him.

The Tory Party Guide to Ireland

Top of the morning to you! As they say in Ireland, a place that, as Northern Ireland Secretary, I do know quite a lot about. I mean, I did know stuff about Ireland before becoming Northern Ireland Secretary: if you'd shown me a map of Ireland, I'd have been able to point straight to Northern Ireland, no messing. It's the bit at the top. But yes, I've also had to learn on the job and now I know it all: *Game of Thrones*, leprechauns, the Easter Rising, the Battle of the Boyne, Thin Lizzy, everything. These days, I'm *all about* the Ireland. I just love the craic! (That's not the same as crack.) (At least, I don't think it is.)

I also now appreciate things like this: that when elections are fought in Northern Ireland, people who are nationalists don't vote for unionist parties and vice versa. Turns out there's this really big division between these two groups going back to, like, the 1990s?

And I also know all about the backstop, the Irish backstop that was designed to keep Britain indefinitely in the customs union as a way of avoiding the reintroduction of a hard border which goes against the Good Friday Agreement [citation needed]. That's a lot of words there, but basically: whenever I see the word 'backstop', I also see the word 'trap'. It's even got the same letters! Apart from the 'r'. And okay, yes, it was a trap the UK government insisted on to try and keep the DUP happy (will the DUP *ever* be happy? I have to speak to them *most days*!). But obviously it's perfectly possible to be tricked into trapping yourself into a trap of your own choosing. It's a trick! *And* a trap! It's the Irish backstop trick-trap!

Anyway, when it comes to so-called 'issues' like the Irish border, the answer has always been so simple: business – specifically, meaning it. Show people you mean business! Get rid of all the negativity. Don't take 'no' for an answer, although I suppose that does slightly depend on what the question was. Thinking about it now, there are probably *some* questions for which 'no' is a fairly reasonable answer. But, in general, don't take 'no' for an answer. Take their 'no' and give them a 'no' in return. That will be another 'no', but it will be *our* 'no', not their 'no'. Saying 'no' to Britain? Fuck off!

Look, when we owned the whole thing, they didn't even *have* a border! Maybe just send in our boys? (What? What have I said *now*?) And, it goes without saying, our girls as well.

Anyway, there's so many fixes on offer these days that I'm actually getting dizzy from all the fixes. Zones. Special zones. Sanitary zones. Phytosanitary zones (the best zones). Drones in the zones. Good drones, not evil ones. Or maybe just evil ones? Killer drones – that'd put the shits up them! Zap them right up! Or lasers ... *space lasers*! Nanobots in the undergrowth. Horses! Horseflies! Leprechauns!

Anyway, gotta go now: *Mrs Brown's Boys* is on. For sure. Fiddle-dee-dee!

Not the face tattoo!

People used to use their faces for telling their stories in the sense of speaking through their mouths. But this was to wildly under-use the actual skin, on the actual face. Luckily, this important medium for solipsistic storytelling has been fully utilised by the recent wave of Soundcloud rappers. You can read them like a book! A shit book.

Lil Xan has his mum's name 'Candy' and his birth year '1996' tattooed onto his face – useful if he ever forgets such personal details when, say, filling out a form. I'm getting my NI number and the name of my first pet done on my tongue. Handy.

Post Malone has the message 'Stay Away' on his face, which presumably he points to if he ever has a bad infection. Under his eyes are the words 'Always Tired'; people often say how ridiculous tattoos will look when the wearers reach old age, but not here! Maybe he's actually planning ahead for when he's slumped in the dayroom, waiting for biscuits?

'Don't chat shit about X!'

That's what people will tell you, if you chat shit about X. They don't like it. So don't do it! They don't mean the letter 'X' but rapper XXXTentacion, who died before revealing the true meanings behind his many, many face tattoos – and also before he was convicted of charges relating to an astonishingly violent case of domestic abuse. You can get XXXTentacion replica fake tattoos, to pay tribute to this hideous figure, still inexplicably beloved by teenage girls. Each to their own, I suppose. These tattoos will include a tree which, according to YouTube commentators, might represent the tree on which he pretended to hang himself in one of his last promo videos. So there's something for Granny to get you for Christmas.

The most infamously stupid face tattoo is, of course, the Anne Frank face tattoo – the really quite surprisingly large Anne Frank face tattoo – sported by the rapper Arnoldisdead. As he explained: 'To be stuck in a house, and end up dying ... dude I'm dying to make music.'

Can you get stupider than that? I'm genuinely not sure that you can.

Unlike the above highly streamed artists, Arnoldisdead's tattoo has rather taken over the whole Arnoldisdead show: he is now sadly just someone whose image people search for when talking about 'that bellend with the Anne Frank face tattoo'. So that's the Arnoldisdead story.

But even sturdier figures can come unstuck when Anne Frank is concerned. The Anne Frank story is, quite famously, her story. She wrote it, about herself. But still people get confused. When Justin Bieber went to the Anne Frank House in Amsterdam, he wrote a comment in the visitors' book: 'Anne was a great girl. Hopefully she would have been a belieber.'

So maybe the Anne Frank story has now become subsumed by a larger, perhaps more resonant story?

Bieber's got face tattoos too, including the word 'Grace'. What can it mean? I think it's a tribute to the legendary English cricketer W. G. Grace: 'Respect going out to my man, Willy G . . . Howzat, bro?!'

How to make it as an influencer: a handy cut-out-and-keep guide (don't actually cut it out, though)

You know you want to. You want to sell your whole self – and indeed your whole soul – to become some weird kind of online shop assistant who's also forever showing snaps of themselves in hotels.

But how?

Invent a new word ending in '. . . fluencer'. Most of the best ones have already been taken. Cleanfluencing is now officially over: anyone still calling themselves a cleanfluencer needs to take a look at themselves in the mirror, the one they've just been wiping for the past four hours. There have also been teenfluencers. Ginfluencers? Done. What about being a stringfluencer? There's so much string out there right now and it can be hard to choose. Or a tinfluencer: being a world expert on tinned foods – useful with panic buying all the rage. Or tin in its raw material state, looking at who's up and who's down in that whole field: Burundi? Bolivia?

There's no such thing as over-sharing. Yes, at the start, it does feel weird to share your life with complete strangers. That's fair: it is weird. But sharing some of those painful childhood memories and then crying in front of the camera for, like, an hour is really, really important for your followers to know the real you and then they'll trust you when you hand out your advice, about cushions.

Get stuff for free. Be warned: you can't just go around asking for free stuff. People *will* tell you to get fucked. At least at first, you do actually have to pay for stuff, both in terms of money and also heartache (but mainly money). But then, after bagging your first 10k or so followers, you'll be getting loads of free stuff. Soon enough, you'll be drowning in free stuff. You'll be surrounded by walls of, say, makeup or toilet paper or matchsticks or cutlery, and you will wonder why. You may cry. Don't worry. It's natural. 'Why am I crying!?!?' Because you're drowning in free soap.

Use your family/pet. Is your pet pulling its weight on social media? Otherwise, what's the point of it? Your tortoise hasn't done anything Instagrammable in days. Does it even *want* to be famous? And your offspring. Seven-year-old Ryan of Ryan ToysReview makes a reported $22m a year from unwrapping and reviewing toys. That could be your little kid that you're sending into this bizarro fame game. Yes, it's your family. But your tribe are sort of your family too. So what if you've never met them, or if you're not even really sure whether they're all spambots. They need you. Don't let them down!

Make a splash. Stunts are an important part of getting noticed ... preferably something dangerous, that might cause hospitalisation. But, failing that, something that leaves everyone wondering whether or not they've just been utterly cheated. Like when the partner of fashion influencer Marissa Fuchs proposed to her on film, and it all looked lovely and real, then it emerged he'd pitched the engagement to brands months beforehand, seemingly seeking to monetise the moment. Did she know? Didn't she know? Would she not have approved anyway? Join the conversation!

Use your influence for evil ... I mean, for *good*! Cleaning products? Really? You actually get up in the morning so you can influence people to buy *cleaning products*? If you do have power over people, at least wield it in an interesting way: like, say, turning your tribe into a full-blown cult? With everyone having shaved their heads? With some huge intermarrying service taking place in some huge amphitheatre somewhere? Yeah, you guys? Would you be super up for that? I'm not saying go full Manson, with your disciples haring down into town on dune buggies armed with bottles of Cif ...

To repeat: I'm saying not to do that. I just wanted to make that clear. I know people are pretty suggestible these days ...

The weaponised rebirth of Russian ultra-nationalism: good or bad? Discuss

In this essay, I am going to examine the weaponised rebirth of Russian ultra-nationalism and ask the question: good or bad? Shall we discuss? Let us discuss.

I shall begin in 2014, when Russia forcibly annexed the contested Ukrainian region of the Crimea. This land-grab was in response to Vladimir Putin's lack of success in regard to the economy, living standards, life expectancy, or anything. Russia was already awash with cults: in 2012, one cult leader, whose followers all worship Vladimir Putin, claimed that an icon of the beloved President had started seeping myrrh. But the Crimean invasion really fired up the weaponised rebirth of Russian ultra-nationalism. Which might be good and might be bad. At this point, we cannot say.

A key figure in this movement is the Orthodox priest Bishop Tikhon, who has been called 'Putin's confessor' and who changed his name – from Georgiy Shevkunov – after what I'd say is a fairly unusual experience with the exhumed corpse of Saint Tikhon, the Patriarch of Moscow who served Tsar Nicholas II (and tussled with the Bolsheviks until his death in 1925). While exploring fire damage at his monastery in 1992, Shevkunov discovered the coffin of his hero. When the lid was lifted, he saw the corpse in a miraculously pristine state. As he later explained, 'Boldly, forgive me God, I put my hand in there with a blessing, and just grabbed the man by the hand and shoulder.'

See what I mean? Unusual, right? After this, Shevkunov renamed *himself* Bishop Tikhon and started a wave of attacks on 'liberal' priests: any Orthodox figures not totally intolerant of gays and Jews. He's also known as the 'Lubyanka Father' for the support he has offered to Russia's retired security officials (that is, torturers and executioners). It's safe to say he has heard a few things in his time.

Additionally, moreover, furthermore, there is Konstantin Malofeev, an ultra-religious oligarch who wants to bring back Tsarism and whose elite academy outside Moscow prepares the elite Russian youth for a future of Tsarist rule. Sending rich sons off to private schools for training in how to lead their nations towards some defining moment of cataclysmic high excitement: do other countries do this? No longer considered a total failure, the last Tsar is now some kind of Russian god. What's more (according to Shevkunov and many others): a Russian god killed by Jews. So this is starting to sound 'not good' at this point, wouldn't you say?

Shevkunov is among many who claim the shooting of the Tsar and his family as a 'ritualistic murder': a medieval term meaning 'Jewish conspiracy'. When Shevkunov criticised *Mathilde,* a controversial 2018 movie about an affair between Tsar Nicholas and the dancer Mathilde Kshesinskaya, an Orthodox activist rammed a minibus into the cinema hosting the premiere. This shouldn't be confused with the stage musical *Matilda*, which I don't think has yet upset any Russian ultra-nationalists.

The movement's iconography also embraces other post-Tsarist figures: one icon, christened by ultra-nationalist writer Alexander Prokhanov, showed Joseph Stalin and his victorious Soviet Second World War generals under a cloud carrying the Virgin and Child. Some Orthodox priests did find equating the mass murderer Joseph Stalin with the Baby Jesus to be a step too far. And maybe it is?

Then there was the diplomatic incident when a pro-Putin ultra-nationalist biker gang set up headquarters on a Slovakian pig farm. The Night Wolves are spreading their influence from Germany to Romania. Poland recently stopped them at the border. So it seems likely that the Poles think that the weaponised rebirth of Russian ultra-nationalism is a *bad* thing.

In addition, furthermore, the Night Wolves worship medieval warrior-monks and are headed by six-foot-three bearded muscle-man Alexander Zaldostanov, a torch bearer at the Sochi Winter Olympics, and also known as The Surgeon. I don't know why The Surgeon is called The Surgeon (I don't want to know why The Surgeon is called The Surgeon).

Consequently, moreover, the Night Wolves frequently put on Christian-patriot bike displays of great Soviet victories from the Second World War, with added Orthodox iconography, and have shared bills with

Steven Seagal's blues band. Steven Seagal really likes Putin (he's an honorary Russian citizen), calling him his 'brother'. So does Gerard Depardieu. And Mickey Rourke. Seagal has said he'd like to become the governor of the far eastern region of Vladivostok. This on top of his part-time job teaching martial arts to the Serbian Special Forces.

So we're dealing with some out-of-the-ordinary situations here. But before reaching a firm conclusion, let's also examine Natalia Poklonskaya, the former Crimean prosecutor general who also treats Tsar Nicholas like a god and also thinks Jews plotted to murder him. ('Many people are afraid to talk about it – but everyone understands that it happened. It is evil.') In 2017, Poklonskaya claimed that the bronze bust of Tsar Nicholas in Simferopol was seen weeping myrrh. The Orthodox Church was sceptical but sent five clergymen to inspect the bust for evidence. (No tears have yet been confirmed.)

When Poklonskaya rose to power in 2014, her photogenic appearance (plus military epaulettes) made her a sensation among Japanese males; many different anime versions of her now exist. One important piece of evidence to examine here is a YouTube video reworking Daft Punk's 'Instant Crush', the original Julian Casablancas vocals replaced by Poklonskaya's own pro-Russian pronouncements. Poklonskaya news footage is cut with scenes of a manga Poklonskaya wielding a sword for Russia before sitting by a river making origami boats and watching them float downstream . . .

Having delineated these key figures, I shall now address the following questions: what the shitting hell is going on? Why is everything so fucking weird? To be honest, it's all getting quite hard to take. Russian ultra-nationalists are annexing my dreams: there's processions of Russian bikers, chanting; the Surgeon is confessing, telling me all he has done for Russia; The Patriarch is in the doorway, beckoning. And the smell of myrrh is *everywhere.*

In conclusion, can I please stop now? I'm starting to regret choosing the Russian Ultra-Nationalism module altogether. I thought it would be fun, but it's not fun.

Are you a toddler?

People who agree with you are great, aren't they? You like that, and give each other Likes.

And people who hold different opinions to you are just doing it to take the piss and get at you, aren't they? And that you do not Like.

What has the Brexit vote proved, besides humanity's unending ability to chase its own tail? It has proved, in spades, that people don't seem to know how to disagree with one another.

They *are* disagreeing – clearly! It would be fun to try

and argue that they aren't, if ultimately futile. They're just not very good at it.

I want it like I want it! Why? Because I want it like I want it!

You don't want to leave the park, do you? And you really want more sweets. Have a wee before getting in the car? Fuck that! I don't even *need* a wee! Bedtime? More Beebies! Want more Beebies!

Plenty has been said about Leavers taken in by the lies of populist leaders and the manipulative propaganda of the data-miners. So let's not rehearse all that again.

Let us consider, instead, what a self-satisfied blether-machine a lot of the Remainers are.

Consider the People's Vote home-made placard (Remainers *love* home-made placards) with the slogan 'WE'RE NOT LEAVING – SO THERE!' The home-made placard equivalent of closing your eyes tightly and claiming therefore that something you don't like doesn't exist. How many Leave voters in, say, Merthyr or Middlesbrough, full square on the shit end of austerity, saw that on the news or the front of the paper and were disabused of the nagging feeling that metropolitan types don't give a toss about them? Because in this People's Vote you were so keen on you'd need more people to vote your way than the last time. That is, to change their minds. Do you actually understand that? I mean, it's just basic maths apart from anything else.

Some things are fairly obviously right – that is,

provably so. Two and two? Four. Some things are obviously wrong. 'If I drop this television off the roof, it will fly upwards into the clouds.' It fucking won't. Some things are more right than other things, or less wrong, while not being definitive. Some things are hypotheses or theories, subject to investigation and possible verification, even if not immediately. And some things are matters of opinion. That is, even if you agree on the facts, you will make a different value judgement. Then you have what is called a Genuine Disagreement. Which exist. And won't fucking kill you.

You may be right about something – but the reason you are right is never because you're special. But how to change other people's minds? Isn't there an app for it? You know, like for ordering takeaways? Or are you not that bothered about changing other people's minds? And just want it like you want it. Because you want it like you want it.

Always have a wee before embarking on a long journey.

And

just

fucking

grow

up.

What historical era does the current era most resemble?

Brexit Britain. Trump's America. *Our Planet.* There's a lot going on these days ... Like, a lot.

People are concerned about the future. And people are also very concerned about the past. But which past? What epoch is our epoch, the so-called current epoch, most like?

What age best sums up our age? Are there lessons to be learned? Could be. There sometimes are.

Austerity Britain?

A time of British pluck in the face of adversity. Just getting on with it. Keeping smiling through. Like an Ealing comedy. But not funny. The Tories have certainly worked their way through Brexit ministers like Dennis Price offing relatives in *Kind Hearts and Coronets. Passport to Pimlico*? With the UK fracturing, we may well soon need passports to enter Pimlico, or Kensington, or Scotland, or Stoke. Watch out, though: *Passport to Pimlico* wasn't even filmed in Pimlico. So fake news there. In 1949. It's like you can't trust *anyone*![2]

---

2 The plot of *Passport to Pimlico* (contains spoilers! Obviously – it's the plot): a group of people split from a larger political body and create a small 'island' to avoid what they see as unnecessary imposed bureaucracy, only to realise they can't survive on their own and eventually have to be bailed out by the people they left in the first place, but by this point are starving and have to give up their one remaining treasure in order to go back to where they started. Only fun.

The 1950s?

UKIP and the Brexit Party love the 1950s – but a 1950s heavy on the powdered egg and far too light on the rock 'n' roll, Angry Young Men-lit explosion and never having had it so good. If they ever got into power, the Brexit Party would go straight back to when things started to go wrong and ban skiffle classic 'Rock Island Line' – specifically to keep The Kids' hands off their most powerful potential weapon: the washboard. Where's me washboard? That's what The Kids would be asking.

The war?

Which war, you ask? Come on: don't take the piss. Brexit Britain is obsessed with Churchill, D-Day and Dunkirk. There has been a major film about Dunkirk, the film *Dunkirk,* and people are always making films about Winston Churchill. You are probably making a film about Winston Churchill right now. Who isn't?

Despite what your gran used to say about all the camaraderie and singalongs, the war was actually quite a terrible time. Some people say: 'We need a war!' We don't, though.

Boris Johnson is a great fan of Churchill. Of course he is. He even wrote a lofty literary biography of Churchill, where he kept slyly equating a Nazi-controlled Europe with the EU. Working Time Directive, Holocaust: same same. *The Churchill Factor: How One Man Made History* it's called. Although I should point out that I read the Nazi EU thing in a review of Mr Johnson's Churchill tome, not the mighty tome itself.

At a push, I could go to the library or a bookshop and double-check. You know, later. But just to be clear: no books by Boris Johnson were purchased in the writing of this book. Not even second hand. (I could even be interested to see what Johnson says about Churchill being ejected in 1945 to be replaced by a radical Labour government. Although, as I say, not interested enough to go all the way to the library. I mean, what if it started raining?)

Anyway, Boris Johnson is keen on learning from history, and so should we be. Those who do not learn from history are doomed to repeat it. And those who do not learn from the history of Boris Johnson are just doomed.

(Note to self: write to the Johnson family suggesting that they all write books about reading each other's books. That wiff-waff table won't pay for itself.)

The Napoleonic Wars?

A long period of war with Europe to maintain Britain's independence. Self-explanatory, this one. We won.

Maybe we should take a page out of the Nelson playbook and send the fleet? You could easily shell Brussels from the Channel. How much would Barnier like a broadside up him? Not much, I expect.

Nelson didn't do it all on his own, of course. He only had one arm, for a start. In fact, the crew of the *Victory*, Nelson's ship at Trafalgar (you knew that), was a motley crew that included – sorry about this – some Frenchmen. *Sacré bleu*!

Why? Er, I'm afraid there was money involved. The crew were all contractually due a share of any booty seized from enemy ships. And they would have indeed been quids in if the booty boat hadn't sunk in a storm on its way back to Blighty.

But anyway, yes – the crew of the *Victory*: economic migrants.

The 1930s?

Everyone is talking about it. The 2010s are the new 1930s. It's not very catchy, but you can see what people mean, what with traditional conservative elites cosying up to nationalist thugs and a general air of incipient disaster. Basically, it's bad. Even just in Britain, it's bad. And it's worse elsewhere. So it's bad.

Labour MP David Lammy got into hot water for comparing the ERG group of Brexiteer Tory MPs to the Nazis. Challenged, he doubled down and said that he hadn't gone far enough. Bloody hell, man.

Tory Lord Heseltine piped up to back Lammy, calling the parallels with the Thirties 'chilling': 'I'm so aware of it because Hitler was elected in Germany in 1933, the day I was born, and so I've always known of this very unfortunate coincidence.

'But the important point is he was elected, and he was elected by all the sort of techniques of thuggery in the democratic process ... And what terrifies me above all is the language I hear from people saying, "Oh, well, if we don't get Brexit, there'll be violence on the streets."'

Tony Blair's former chief of staff Jonathan Powell said, in a piece for BBC's *This Week*, that Britain risks 'ending up like the Weimar Republic' – by which he means collapsing and being replaced by fascism, not lots of experimental theatre and saucy cabarets.

Although burlesque is still quite popular. So, er, look on the bright side, mate?

The Corn Laws?

The Conservative Party is the world's oldest political party and often called the most 'successful' political party, too. But our natural leaders shafted themselves sideways in the 1840s, in a vicious disagreement about corn. The battle over the so-called Corn Laws, which were laws concerning corn, saw the Tories split and crash out of power for the next 28 years. The laws were brought in after the Napoleonic Wars, which we won, to protect British corn (British corn: best corn in the world) – and in particular big (mainly Tory) landowners – from an influx of cheap foreign corn, for example from Poland (for good builders, think corn). The victors of Waterloo were having none of it. So in 1815 the government slapped tariffs on the hated foreign corn.

Over time, the artificially high price of bread led to rioting and, to stem the rise of the Brexit Party – sorry, pro-free trade Anti-Corn Law League – Prime Minister Robert Peel pushed through abolition of the Corn Laws in 1846 in defiance of most of his party, relying on opposition Whig MPs to 'get the deal done'. Tory 'ultras' resigned from the Cabinet and the party split. With the economy tanking (demand was low, as people had to spend all their bread on bread), Peel put country before party. Just get on with it? He did.

Both tariffs and corn are still hot potatoes. Corn is big: it's in cornflakes, high-fructose corn syrup and corn on the cob (I mean, that's literally *just corn*). To this day, people still eat bread. Maybe they always will?

Tax-free corn? What are you, some sort of anarchist? Just get on with it!

The 1970s?

A time of strife. But also a time when apparently people were statistically happiest – even notwithstanding all the chip pan fires.

The 1980s?

Right versus left for the soul of the country. Rees-Mogg versus Corbyn! This theory was given credence when Paul Weller came out of political retirement to do a Red Wedge-style benefit gig for Corbyn – like a sort of left-wing King Arthur returning from the misty political yonderlands in the Left's time of need. That's Weller, not Corbyn. Corbyn had always been here.

The 1980s also gave birth to the idea that small states and deregulated markets mean prosperity and happiness for all. How's that one working out for you?

The 1960s?

A lot of technology about, so there's that – except tech isn't white hot now as you can't even see data, let alone take its temperature. And the news does often look like a Peter Blake montage or auto-destructive art Happening. What's it all about, Alfie? That is the question.

The 1990s?

Nope. No one gives a flying fuck about the 1990s. Apart from people watching the *Trainspotting* sequel, but only for the duration of the film and the time just before and after watching it spent crapping on, to anyone who'll listen, about how much they used to 'Ave It.

The conspiracy of silence on the anniversary of

Blair's election was extraordinary (practically no one was talking about it): like a mass unconscious effort to forget. 'Remember when we elected that bullshitter and he marketised education and did some wars and it all ended in a huge financial crash?' 'No.' 'No, me neither. Shhh.'

Even Noel Gallagher (who, by his own admission, 'won the '90s'), charged with remixing Oasis's famously, er, baggy third album *Be Here Now* for an anniversary Director's Cut, hoping to slash it down to size, managed one single afternoon in the studio listening to the master tapes before just, well, walking out and going home declaring he had 'fookin' better things to do with me time. *Tipping Point*'s on in a bit.'

It's his album, and he could only be arsed to listen to it through, like, once. He's had it with the '90s.

The 780s?

Brexit is very, very like the shenanigans between Mercian king Offa and Frankish king Charlemagne. But you knew that.

There are some differences. The Tories have not yet dug a massive dyke between England and Wales (that's their next major project). But the (partial) ruler of England and the (partial) ruler of Europe got into hot diplomatic water when a planned merger (or 'union') – a marriage between the former's daughter and the latter's son – fell through after Offa realised this might lead to a European super-state.

Offa's ships were forbidden from landing in Charlemagne's ports, thus causing a logjam in European trade – there were carts all the way up the M20!

The Victorian era, generally?

Should we make a return to the days of moral fibre, sturdy underwear and civic vim? Some people have argued thus, saying we should rediscover the grim determination of this long-ago golden age. Jacob Rees-Mogg, meanwhile, unleashed his book *The Victorians*, about the Victorians. It is fair to say the book divided critics – between those who hated it and those who really hated it. (It was variously called 'abysmal', 'soul-destroying' and 'reads like it was written by a baboon'.)

Rees-Mogg was just asking for trouble, though, with such a bold reappraisal of the Victorian age and his attempt to draw out contemporary resonances. He focused on 'twelve titans who forged Britain'. Not all that radical, you might think, until you see which twelve titans he chose as his twelve titans: William Cufay the Black Chartist leader, Gentleman Jack (an lesbian), Mary Seacole (an nurse), William Morris socialist and wallpaper enthusiast, Keir Hardie, Charles Dickens, John Ruskin ('Life should be beautiful. Nanny always said that but little did I know she was quoting Mr

Ruskin! . . .'), Oscar Wilde, J. M. W. Turner ('I thought he was just a character in one of my beloved Mike Leigh films but no – turns out he was real!'), Percy Bysshe 'Red' Shelley, Karl Marx ('immigrants are Brits too!') and music hall saucepot Marie Lloyd ('A very rude lady! In a good way').

Ha! Not really. He just crapped on about obvious whiskery Victorian bigwigs (Queen Victoria was the only woman to make the cut), trying to pretend they'd have loved nothing more than a No Deal Brexit and Jacob Rees-Mogg in the Cabinet. Pull yourself up by your bootstraps and keep your tackle to yourself – that was the theme here. The Empire was of course a splendid and noble endeavour resulting in eternal gratitude from our colonial 'charges' (yes, he does use that word). Even A. N. Wilson, someone so into Victorian stuff that he actually is a Victorian, called *The Victorians* 'staggeringly silly'.

A Britain of grinding poverty and the iron rule of one's betters? I simply cannot imagine it.

By the way, check out Jacob Rees-Mogg's show on LBC: he plays some *tunes*! (He doesn't. It's talk radio. You knew that.)

So which era are we reliving now? I think it's all the above, and more too. History repeats itself, it has been suggested – first time as tragedy, second time as farce. And third time as Brexit. Third time lucky? You decide.

New football stadiums: shit

Do Spurs deserve to play inside a spaceship? Shouldn't they have at least won something first?

It is presumably no coincidence that the brilliantly named Tottenham Hotspur Stadium is the largest of all the London teams' stadiums, reflecting the club's ambitions. Which are to be much more successful than they now are. Their ambitions are quite simply nothing less than to achieve actual things. They've had it with having potential.

The new massive stadium means plenty of room for that all-important trophy cabinet. Just as there is plenty of room inside the trophy cabinet (boom!).

Bars, swanky bars, swankier bars. Shiny things! The stadium is topped with a glass walkway, where visitors can walk out to touch a massive cock. And surrounded by lots of new houses and retail units. Go sports!

It is both 'the best stadium in the world' (stick that, Real! Jealous much, Bayern?) and 'a benchmark of how stadiums should be designed' – according to the architects.

The same architects also designed Arsenal's stadium. Which might not bode well. Since moving to the Emirates in 2006, Arsenal, the former 'Invincibles', have only won the FA Cup – the latter stages and final of which you play *somewhere else*. They have won it three times, to be fair, but won nothing else: it is a perfect illustration of the shitness of new football stadiums. Arsenal left the glory days behind when they left Highbury, coincidentally the only ground Jay Gatsby would ever have been seen dead in.

Even teams who do quite well in new stadiums find their fans don't like it anyway. Man City have empty seats at home games at the Etihad. Whereas St James's Park is full to bursting despite Newcastle last winning a major trophy in 1969. And, even then, it was the Fairs Cup, a long-forgotten forerunner to the currently forgotten Europa League that started as a competition only open to cities hosting trade fairs. (No disrespect intended. To the Toon or, er, trade fairs.)

Is it not time to get back to basics? Chopper Harris, mud, fags at half time. Goalposts for goalposts. It's not football if you can see what's happening clearly. People at the football should only be eating vari-temperatured mush contained within low-grade pastry, not accessing the high-speed broadband while munching burritos.

Or utilising the ample toilet facilities. You're not a real fan, it's oft said, until you've reached into your pocket at a match and fished out a pie sodden – literally sodden – with another man's piss. And yes, it could be argued that in the all-seating era the practice of giving someone a so-called 'hot leg' by unburdening yourself of your nine pints of pre-match mild into their pocket is, well, unnecessary.

But just because it's not necessary is not a reason *in itself* not to do something.

Please yourself on that front, but undersoil heating? Fuck off.

The old Wembley might have been beyond shit – the sightlines were awful, there was a track around the pitch, which was miles from the stands, pillars blocked the view everywhere, and it was always full of fucking England fans – but it did look good on telly. The pitch was huge and other-worldly, a green stage floating in space. It looked like no other stadium in the country. A special place for special occasions. The most famous of all, of course, being the one memorably described in 1966 by BBC commentator Kenneth Wolstenholme ... 'Yes, it's Wednesday's cup!' he confidently announced when Sheffield Wednesday went two up in that year's cup final. Wednesday eventually lost 3–2 to Everton. Kenneth Wolstenholme was always saying shit like that.

At the turn of the millennium, Wembley was razed to the ground and replaced with a tin warehouse that makes your local branch of Staples look like Chartres Cathedral. Similar sub-lavvy structures sprang up around the land as beloved idiosyncratic stadiums were bulldozed: Derby's higgledy-piggledy old Baseball Ground, where Cloughie used to sip the chairman's whisky until he changed the locks on the drinks cabinet; and the Dell, Southampton's model-village-sized monument to disorder.

It's not like Spurs had been having to play in the park

or anything. Their old stadium, the rubbishly named White Hart Lane, was one of a series of classic British stadiums designed by the brilliantly named Archibald Leitch. It too had a massive cock on it.

Glaswegian Leitch was responsible for much of the classic going-to-the-match look and feel of British football during its imperial between-the-wars phase. He designed some very fancy stands indeed for the big clubs of the time: Arsenal, Aston Villa, Everton, Chelsea, Liverpool, Sunderland, Blackburn Rovers and (ask Granny) Manchester United.

Leitch's masterpiece was the main stand at Ibrox, home of popular ecumenical concern Rangers. In those days clubs sensibly invested their money in marble, stained-glass windows and sweeping staircases with baroque wooden banisters, rather than wasting it on paying the players.

In later years, having achieved all his architectural ambitions, Archibald Leitch famously changed his name to Cary Grant and conquered Hollywood. His daughter is Carrie Grant off of BBC1's *Fame Academy* (all true: you can check if you want) (but there's no need).

Old Trafford – it's even got the word 'Old' in its actual name and it's literally falling down and infested with rats. That's more like it!

Old football stadiums: shit

Old football stadiums are shit: all you can get to eat is botulism and they smell like toilets.

Old Trafford? If you sit in the crumbling Sir Bobby Charlton stand, you get wet if it rains because of the massive fucking hole in the fucking roof. It's infested with rats!

Yeah, the Glazers are reportedly in the market for a couple of tins of paint, so Old Trafford should get a lick soon. But it's not enough for the modern game.

You want to stop spending money on players and at least get some marble down. Think of how much stained glass you spaffed on Alexis Sanchez alone!

Football's moved on. It's not all big blokes pushing each other over when they think the ref's not looking and shin-kicking festivals any more. People want their high-speed wi-fi and their high-speed wi-fi they must have.

Old Trafford? It's self-parodic.

Haven't you seen Spurs' new stadium? It's like a fucking spaceship. I'm sure 'Lads, it's Tottenham' was one of your lines?

Prawn sandwiches? Not even the half of it. They've got loaded flatbreads and Malaysian Rendang.

You want to raise your fucking game.

Mini-Trumps: Assemble

Mini-Trumps are normal-sized Trump's most hardcore elected supporters – as in headlines like 'Meet the Mini-Trump candidates hoping to storm the US midterms' and 'Mini-Trumps increase stranglehold on Republican Party'. Together they form a phalanx of Trumpian warriors, travelling the land in their Trump's-face blimp, spreading race hate, each one representing a different facet of the President's personality . . .

First, there is Race-Baiter Mini-Trump, Steve King, who keeps a Confederate flag on his desk and once referred to immigration as a 'slow-motion Holocaust' – in three words being both offensively anti-immigrant and offensively anti-Semitic. Well, at least he's concise. At a recent rally, Trump said of avowed white supremacist King: 'He may be the world's most conservative human being.' So that's him.

Then there's Hypocrite Mini-Trump: Tennessee Congressman Scott DesJarlais is a former doctor who is very strongly anti-abortion, although his first wife did have two abortions during their marriage and he allegedly urged a patient with whom he had an affair to have an abortion during a pregnancy scare (it turned out she wasn't even pregnant). And she was far from being the only person with whom he broke the patient-doctor contract in a sex way (he was fined by the Tennessee Board of Medical Examiners). 'God has forgiven me,' he later claimed. God has so far not confirmed the truth of this statement.

Next we come to Having Issues With The Whole 'Course Of Justice' Thing Mini-Trump, Matt Gaetz, who sent tweets attacking Trump's ex-lawyer Michael Cohen while Cohen was on trial for campaign fund violations (on behalf of Trump's campaign). In one tweet, Gaetz leeringly suggested that Cohen's wife would not remain faithful while Cohen was incarcerated for his (Trump-related) crimes. Some members of Congress believed that this and other anti-Cohen tweets were a clear case of witness tampering. Gaetz denied this, saying he was merely 'witness testing, not witness tampering'. Hey, come on, I was just testing him! Right before testing whether he can float with cement shoes on ...

Which is where we come to Suck Up To The Powerful Mini-Trump. One 2018 campaign ad showed Florida governor Ron DeSantis with his young daughter, building a wall with cardboard bricks and reading her *The Art of the Deal* by Donald Trump. Helped other Florida parents indoctrinate their own kids by using public money to provide vouchers for 14,000 families to spend on private education – including the privately run religious school in Orlando where he announced the scheme.

Let us not forget Hyper-Litigious Mini-Trump Devin Nunes, another rabid right-winger who launched a defamation lawsuit seeking $250m in damages against Twitter for allowing accounts under the names 'Devin Nunes' Mom' and 'Devin Nunes' Cow' (he used to be a dairy farmer). Inevitably, these fake accounts quickly gained more followers than Nunes' own, and the court case took a further self-defeating turn when Nunes' lawyer failed to use the account holders' real names in his complaint, leading to statements like: 'In her endless barrage of tweets, Devin Nunes' Mom maliciously attacked every aspect of Nunes' character, honesty, integrity, ethics and fitness to perform his duties as a United States Congressman ... Devin Nunes' Mom ... falsely accused Nunes of being a racist, [and] having "white supremacist friends."' Devin Nunes' Mom has so far not confirmed the truth of this statement.

Texan Congressman Louie Gohmert is Climate Change-Denying Mini-Trump. He said that global warming isn't happening and anyway, if it was, which it isn't, it would be good as it would lead to 'more plants'. He also once claimed terrorists were sending women to the US to have babies who would then be trained abroad before being sent back to attack America. Which is a pretty Trumpian thing to say, all in all.

Taking Things Too Far Mini-Trump Paul Gosar rejected normal-sized Trump's uncharacteristically even-handed characterisation of the trouble at the Unite the Right white supremacist rally in Charlottesville where an anti-fascist protestor was killed ('very fine people on both sides') by saying the whole thing was a false flag put-up job staged by Democrats, funded by George Soros (of course), who for good measure he accused of collaborating with the Nazis during the war.

Threatening People With Violence Mini-Trump Greg Gianforte hit the headlines when he hit a reporter at a rally and then lied about it. While standing for the Montana seat in Congress, Gianforte 'body-slammed' *Guardian* journalist Ben Jacobs, sending him crashing to the floor, then jumped on him. Jacobs said: 'He whaled on me once or twice ... He got on me and I think he hit me.' Gianforte still got elected. Of course he did. Normal-sized Trump called him 'my guy'. He was convicted of assault.

But at least Gianforte wasn't armed. Perhaps most dangerous of all these little guys is Enemy Of Democracy Mini-Trump, Georgian governor Brian Kemp, who accused his black female Democrat opponent of being a George Soros (him again!)-backed liar. Kemp's 'reforms' of the electoral register saw 53,000, mostly African-American, people's right to vote put on hold. He is, however, surprisingly liberal when it comes to immigration ... not really! In his 2018 re-election ads, he was filmed holding a rifle and sitting in a pick-up truck 'just in case I need to round up criminal illegals and take them home myself'. Since his victory, he hasn't actually followed through on these promises to abduct undocumented immigrants and dispense truck-related justice – you know what it's like: they act one way when they're campaigning and another when they're in office – but the clip is undoubtedly what might be termed 'a bit lynchy'.

So, in summary: even when it's over, it won't be. It's like *Gremlins*, but with hard-right, anti-feminist, race-baiting arseholes.

A Future Lexicon: as in, a lexicon of the Future not a lexicon only for reading later on for some reason

Advertising. The point of the Internet?

Artificial Intelligence. Google CEO Sundar Pichai said that Artificial Intelligence will have a more profound effect on the world than electricity or fire. But what if we turned off all the electricity and then set fire to all the computers? (Don't put that in Google, though – don't let the machines know!)

Augmented Reality. Something that many people think will be great but will most likely be irritating as fuck. AR is the overlaying of the digital universe on to the real one, so they merge. Text and pictures will appear before your eyes, or in your headset (or your Google Glasses: remember them? No, no one does): text, images, information about who you are talking to (and adverts, always the adverts) . . . So, yes, just like in all those films. Essentially, imagine if the whole world was Pokemon Fucking Go. *All* the fucking time.

Batteries. A lot of great alleged future tech relies on the development of batteries that don't yet exist. 'Then we just store the energy over there, in mumble

mumble mumble . . .' 'What?' 'We store it in the cough cough.' 'Are you promising to store energy in batteries that don't exist again?' 'Little bit.' 'We've talked about this . . .'

Big Data. You know what They already do with your data: ads, Cambridge Analytica, GCHQ/NSA, surveillance capitalism, weird YouTube recommendations and such? Like that, but with even bigger computers crunching even more of your data and then interacting with your data to create more data, and then interacting with that, and so on. And so on. And so on. And so on. Starting: before.

Cloning. I looked into this in depth by watching the classic Gregory Peck/Laurence Olivier film *The Boys from Brazil*, and what I found is that in the classic film *The Boys from Brazil* a cabal of escaped Nazis led by Josef Mengele breed a load of clones of Hitler. That's some serious shit right there. I'm not down with breeding a load of Hitlers. That sort of trouble we just do not need. The film raises lots of important questions. The Nazis are based in Paraguay, for a start – so why is it called *The Boys from Brazil*? And other, potentially more important questions. Should we clone Hitler? No. That kind of trouble we just do not need. So far, the Brits have cloned sheep and the Chinese have cloned macaques. Funky monkeys I'm okay with, I think. And sheep are mostly all right. But not – I'm unwaverable on this – Hitler.

The Cloud. A beautiful name for a beautiful way of

handing over all your beautiful data without reading the beautiful Terms or beautiful Conditions, as per.

Consciousness. Not telling. Shhh.

Cryptocurrency. Good or bad? Well, it's money, so you work it out. Anyway, there are optimists who think that Blockchain (it means digital transactions carrying a 'block' saying where it has come from and what it has interacted with, permanently held on numerous computers) will herald a new era of a free, peer-to-peer Internet, finishing off Big Data, Big Tech, Big Brother and all the Other Big Bad Big Things Yet To Be Conjured Up. Want a book? Pay the author! Money to invest? Don't go to the bank. The bank will just take you to the cleaners. No middlemen! No PayPal, even! Most of the Bitcoin (there's a finite amount) is *already* concentrated in a few hands, though – so, er . . .

And then there's Libra, Facebook's new cryptocurrency. Zuckerberg's beautiful dream is and was always to 'connect everyone' (on the planet). To each other, yes – but also to him, and his adverts. Facebook tries to keep people off the Internet outside Facebook, the better to monopolise their data. Having their own currency is a logical step.

Is Facebook a country? It has its own law, and its own currency . . . it has 2.4bn people: a 'population' far bigger than any actual country. 'Where are you from?' 'Facebook.' You'll be able to spend the shitly named Libra elsewhere too (of course).

Amazon and Alibaba are also moving into financial services. Of course they are. International banking authorities said it would imperil the stability of the global financial system. Of course they did. But will Blockchain come to the rescue and bring about the end of the middlemen, shady bank deals and the men of means? Historically, middlemen, shady bankers and the men of means have proved quite resilient. As have net billionaires.

Data. You. Your essence. Your '-ness'. A study released in autumn 2018 calculated that more than 90 per cent of all the world's data at that time had been created in the previous two years. Think about that. And see also Big Data (to recap: like data, only more so, already happened).

Deepfake. Deepfake image synthesis uses computer graphics and AI to construct images, and video, that are very, very hard to establish as fakes. (And this technology will only advance, as things tend to.) Recent deepfake 'triumphs' include one of US House Speaker and Democrat Nancy Pelosi making her sound pissed-up – which was frenziedly shared by Trumpites – and shitloads of Trump and Kim K ones, natch. And a splendid one, by some artists (artists, eh?) and an ad agency (watch them like hawks), that had a convincingly doctored Mark Zuckerberg intoning: 'Imagine this for a second . . . One man with total control of billions of people's stolen data, all their secrets, their lives, their futures . . .'

Which of course left Facebook with a dilemma: would they take it down? Could they host all the future deepfakes – and all those hits and thus sweet, sweet ads – if they 'censored' this one? Equally, could they be seen as serious about cracking down on untruthful content (ha!) if they left it up? But old Zuck's a good sport (ha!) so they left it up, albeit unpromoted and as effectively buried as they could get away with.

Why believe something that looks real is a fake? Why believe something real isn't a fake, given all the fakes about – and all the people you don't like and/or agree with? Human credulity's rep is not riding high at the mo. So, er, great.

DeepMind Health. When Google/Alphabet Inc bought an AI company organising NHS data they promised to keep it independent and at arm's length. When Google then shortly afterwards absorbed the company into its own structures (and who – who? – could have predicted that?), it then promised not to link people's health records to their Google accounts or to abuse the data. Will they? Have they? Who can say?

Who can't say any more is the independent panel that had been set up to monitor DeepMind Health when it won the contracts in the first place – as the panel ceased to exist when Google absorbed the company, because the company no longer existed. Just to be clear, the patients still existed, and so did their data – it's just the panel tasked with protecting them that ceased to exist. Were we witnessing, in the words of Julia Powles, research fellow at New York University's School of Law, 'a subsidiary of Google/Alphabet just brazenly lying for years and then handing over the gold to their patron'? Who can say?

Dopamine. The point of the Internet?

Driverless cars. Not all that. They can't operate in snow, or even heavy rain, as they can't 'see' the road markings they need to navigate. They will reduce congestion as people will car-share? Er, no – people aren't down with sharing, apparently. Faceless robot driver? Fine. Human strangers? Fuck off.

Crucially, though – and this is a 'kicker scenario', surely? – they can't drive. Merging into traffic, particularly at speed on, say, a motorway – you know, where merging is A Thing – AI simply can't replicate the human brain's wildly complex combination of custom, practice and real-time assessment of whether some twat is going to slow down or not. They also get totally confused by busy cities. That is, cities. They can't even lean out of the window to give people who cut them up the bird. They won't chase them to the next set of lights and call them a massive dick and then roll the window up when they get of the car and are much bigger than they'd thought.

Driverless motorbikes. In 2019, Facebook lodged designs for self-driving robot motorbikes – claiming they would help cut traffic congestion, taking up less space than cars. They hadn't just rewatched *Tron* or anything.

5G. How many Gs do we actually need, at the end of the day? Pretty sure I was fine with three. Couldn't even tell you what the fourth one is, let alone the fifth. Stardust? Myrrh? It's like razors that keep needlessly adding blades. I can shave quite successfully already!/ watch clips of Mr Beast and the Vlogsquad on my phone already! – so, er, don't bother?

Flying cars. Not going to happen. How would it work? Loads of cars randomly flying about in the sky? Just look at the Star Wars prequel *Attack of the Clones*. It's fucking stupid! Flying cars, that is, not the film. But also the film.

The Fourth Industrial Revolution. Is the Fourth Industrial Revolution actually a real Industrial Revolution? The Third one was supposed to be computers. And this is just more computers, surely?

Bigger computers. More computers. More independent computers.

But computers.

Typical messianic tech nerds, trying to nab two Industrial Revolutions for themselves. Good job you can't buy Industrial Revolutions or they'd have millions of the bastards. (To be fair, the first two were pretty similar, too. Steam/water-powered factories versus electricity-powered, more efficient factories: still factories, innit? Making stuff rather than just growing it.)

The nerds try to make their so-called Fourth Industrial Revolution more distinctive by adding in gene editing and that kind of thing. And, yes, at the point they can invent living things then that might – might – be grounds for them to claim another Industrial Revolution for themselves.

But they can't, so they shouldn't. They are and remain very much just a part of what is, as I think we've established, the Second Industrial Revolution.

Gene editing/genetic enhancement. If recent breakthroughs in mussing with genes/the genome (your genetic recipe for, er, you) lead (eventually) to the ability to have super-babies genetically boosted to have greater abilities, or apply genetic enhancements to existing people to boost *their* abilities, will the tech billionaires, and the super-rich generally, totally do that?

Rhetorical question, obviously. Who wants a shit baby?

Global catastrophic risks. Sound bad, are bad. You're aware of climate change and the robots? Don't forget asteroids hitting the Earth, plagues, pandemics, terrorism, volcanic eruptions or nuclear Armageddon! Or anything else that might 'inflict serious damage to human well-being on a global scale'. But it's okay ... the Future of Humanity Institute in Oxford – who provided that definition – are on it, beavering away at how humanity can get its collective shit together before the shit goes down. Professor Nick Bostrom calls the race to keep up with AI 'philosophy with a deadline'. It's an excellent coining. But also something of an admission that he hasn't divined The Answer yet. Come on, Bostrom, stop pissing about all day: just get on with it!

Go. An game. In fact, Go – a thousands-of-years-old Chinese game – is considered to be the most difficult board game in the world. Not like Monopoly or Risk, which just take a long time, or Operation, which is fiddly, but *well* tricky: trickier than chess. Lots of thinking and that.

They said computers couldn't beat humans at chess. But they did. Well, they would though, wouldn't they? Of course they would. In chess, a player typically has a choice of 20 moves. In Go, it's 200. There are more possible positions in Go than atoms in the universe. Gin rummy it is not.

So they said computers couldn't beat humans at Go. But in a public match with Chinese Go Master Lee Se-Dol in Seoul in 2017, an AI programme thrashed the puny human 3–0 in a best-of-five contest.

AlphaGo had taught itself to play Go by studying footage of human matches and playing with itself (hur hur, I said playing with itself). People were astounded by the machine's decisive public victory.

Thing is, though: maybe the twat just got lucky?

Google buses. The name given to the wi-fi enabled buses that illegally used San Francisco public bus stops to ferry Silicon Valley types to, er, Silicon Valley. The buses were laid on to shield Silicon Valley types from the effect they were having on the city: spiralling rents leading to homelessness, foodbank queues, drugs, prostitution and violent crime. The city legalised their use of the bus stops. So that's all right.

Google Cities. Smart cities, where everything is connected and data is all around (cities 'built from the Internet up'), are on their way. Of course they are. And Google are up to their necks in it. Of course they are. They just want to help, as per.

And also, in the words of Dan Doctoroff, CEO of Google/Alphabet smart city company Sidewalk Labs: 'We're in this business to make money.' Of course they are.

Google tracking you at all times, even when you're not consciously interacting with Google: is that good? Anyway, it's already happened. A trial in Toronto was not well received. People were uneasy at public space being handed over, in total, to a private company, calling it a 'land grab' on their data. And their land. Would the riverside development be 'the coolest new neighborhood on the planet – or a peek into the Orwellian metropolis that knows everything about everyone?' The jury's out! Like anything else you might worry about, the Chinese have already done it, too, only more so – with Cloud Town, a beautiful name for a beautiful way to, etc. ... And so on ... again.

Huawei. Pronounced Huaweiweiwei. Wei. When the 5G (whatever that is) security fuss kicked off, Huawei boss Peter Zhou said American politicians and officials are 'ignorant of technology' and that he often had to 'explain it to them like I do to my kids'. After a public outcry, the UK decided not to trust the network to China. Although it had been happy to commission them to, say, build nuclear power stations, presumably computer-controlled ones. Heard of hacking much? Not that you generally have to hack something you yourself built. But still.

Immortality. The point of Internet billionaires? If the onward march of tech power reached the point where humans could upload their consciousness to a supercomputer and live forever as so-called transhumans, potentially enhancing and extending their organic selves or – fuck it – just leaving them behind, will the tech billionaires, and the super-rich generally, totally do that?

Rhetorical question? It's not like they're already paying to be cryogenically frozen when they 'die'. Oh, hang on . . .

The Internet of Things. Every fucking thing in the world connected to the Internet. So your fridge can keep GCHQ and the Chinese up to date on your milk consumption. Thing is, can anyone say truthfully that, when their fridge texts them to say their milk has turned, they won't then take the milk out and sniff it, to check – just like they would have done anyway? WASTE OF EVERYONE'S FUCKING TIME.

JEDI (Joint Enterprise Defence Contract). It was widely believed that Google's Project Maven, the provision of map technology to improve the accuracy of military drones, was an audition to bag JEDI, the $10bn contract that's probably the largest IT procurement in history. The company was forced to pull out of the race when its employees protested: apparently, facilitating war was just a little *too* hard to square with the whole 'do no evil' thing.

Former Google CEO Eric Schmidt is still head of a Pentagon committee designed to integrate Silicon Valley into the intelligence services. Amazon and Microsoft are also still trying to land the JEDI contract to provide a cloud computing system that can 'network American forces all over the world and integrate them with AI'. What could possibly go wrong? Automising the world's greatest war machine under the control of a network of computers? And *of course* you can trust nerdy warlords who create an all-encompassing war machine and make its acronym JEDI. Oh no, hang on – you absolutely fucking can not.

Memes. Things that catch on. The wheel. Fire. The Muslim crescent. The Christian cross. Memes all. The term was coined by Richard Dawkins in his book *The Selfish Gene*, which is about how wild cats evolved into housecats and then subsequently into cats that do things so humorous – wearing a hat, say – that, not only will you laugh out loud, but your mum and all your friends will too. Atheism and lol-cats: that's old Dawkins.

Minerals. Boffins at the University of Plymouth have

calculated that, to create one smartphone, 10–15kg of ore has to be mined, including 'conflict' elements such as tungsten and cobalt that come from unregulated mines in dictatorial, child-labour utilising Democratic (ha!) Republic (ha!) of (not ha! literally just a preposition, and best of luck to it generally) Congo (not ha! that's literally just a place name. Fucking river, innit). At least 1.4 billion smartphones are made every year. The Plymouth boffins worked out which elements were in the smartphone by putting it in a blender. It didn't work afterwards.

Preppers. It's easy to dismiss as overkill the people preparing for social breakdown by laying in tinned food and medicines, learning to hunt, forage and fish, and getting tooled up (with guns, and also actual tools) in remote locations – until you hear about the sort of people taking this kind of thing deadly seriously.

Antonio García Martínez, who made a fortune selling his online ad company to Twitter and then took a senior role at Facebook, wrote an insider's account of Silicon Valley movers and shakers: *Chaos Monkeys*. And now he spends most of his time on a remote settlement, accessible only by 4×4, on an island off the coast of Washington State. Generator? Check. Compost toilet? Check. Guns? Check check check. 'I've seen what's coming ... I think we could have some very dark days ahead of us,' he told author Jamie Bartlett. Right-wing libertarian PayPal billionaire Peter Thiel (him again!) has taken New Zealand citizenship and bought a massive plot of land there in Wanaka; apparently, 'buying a house in New Zealand' is winking super-rich code for 'building a bunker for the apocalypse in New Zealand'.

LinkedIn co-founder Reid Hoffman told the *New Yorker* in 2017 that half of all Silicon Valley billionaires have some level of 'apocalypse insurance', and discuss survivalist techniques on secret, closed Facebook groups: gold, guns, escape routes – all of that. So the people building the future fear the chaos that they may themselves unleash. Chaos Monkeys. Especially chaotic monkeys. Hmm. Chaos Monkeys with guns? Great.

Privacy. Very much a thing of the past.

Regulation. Google spends more on lobbying than any other US company. All the Big Tech companies are desperate to avoid regulation, because they need to be free to innovate and anyway are completely benign. Not because they just want to make a shitload of cash and not give any of it to the government or be told to stop doing stuff because other people – normies! – say it's harmful.

They also say they are the people best placed to keep an eye on their own activities, be it developing AI or monitoring content on their platforms, because they know what they're doing and the government does not (because they won't tell it). Someone saying there is something that needs to be watched and that they are just the people to do the watching, what with them being what needs watching in the first place. It makes some logical sense, of course: who is better placed to know what someone is up to than the person who is up to it? What could possibly go wrong? In a word: Cambridge Analytica, etc. Okay, that's three words.

Sex robots. Robots you can have sex with. Fairly self-explanatory, that one. While also sort of not. In a recent survey, 40 per cent of British men said they would have sex with a robot, while 50 per cent of Americans would totally have it off with a saucebot, and so would 52 per cent of Germans. Germans literally making love to engineering. Will some people fall in love with their sex robot? Of course they fucking will.

The Singularity. The point where technology becomes so clever, and self-developing, that we simply cannot understand it and must merge with it or bow down to it. Might not happen for ages. Might have already happened. A frog in gradually boiling water scenario if ever there was one.

Smart toilets. Smart washing machine? Of course. Smart trousers that help the elderly, for example, to stand up and move about? Why not? But a smart toilet? No. How fucking smart does a toilet need to be? It's literally a pipe you shit down.

Synthetic bioengineering. Engineering and biology: together at last! Breaking all the rules. By, er, using the techniques of engineering to muss with natural stuff. The boffins are aiming to be able to do nothing less than be creators of life – aren't they always? – but have so far only managed to move the odd bit of DNA about. Still, keep an eye on them. Amateurs are having a crack at it, too. So-called biohackers. Doesn't sound good, does it, bio-hacking? So keep an eye on what your geeky neighbour is up to in their spare room, too. They could – could – be building a man.

Tech billionaire parenting. Steve Jobs strictly rationed his kids' use of tech. Bill and Melinda Gates' kids aren't even allowed smartphones and are only allowed to use a computer in the kitchen. The most sought-after private school in Silicon Valley, the Waldorf School of the Peninsula (Mark Zuckerberg's kids go there, as do the progeny of the Uber, eBay and Apple barons) (it's a hell of a name for a school, mind), bans electronic devices for under-11s and encourages the kids to play outside, build go-karts, cook and knit. Knitting? That may backfire when they're older. Also, only in the kitchen? You'd think the Gates house would be big enough to include a study.

Technological solutionism. A term coined by tech thinker Evgeny Morozov to describe the nerds' belief that everything is ultimately computable and thus solv-able by technology. Complex social issues are reframed as 'neatly defined problems with definite, computable solutions ... if only the right algorithms are in place!' Your algorithm is causing havoc? You just need another algorithm to sort out the first algorithm. (Have they not heard about the old woman who swallowed a fly? That didn't go well.)

The Internet giveth, but the Internet doth not taketh away: cyber-utopianism. Hmm. Even benign techies should be kept an eye on: in his book *Ten Arguments for Deleting Your Social Media Accounts Right Now*, Virtual Reality and Internet pioneer Jaron Lanier bemoans the techies' certainty that their on-off/one-zero logic could be applied to all things (like, say, human society), discussing how the Internet was built without a way to make or get payments – i.e., pay for content, like writing or music – or a way to find other people you might like and want to connect or cooperate with. 'Everyone knew these functions ... would be needed. We figured it would be wiser to let entrepreneurs fill in the blanks than to leave that task to government ... We foolishly laid the foundations for global monopolies.' Those monopolies have created a 'hell', says Lanier, of multinational corporations 'twitch[ing] our marionette strings'.

Was this laissez-faire attitude to laissez-faire naivety at the level – given, you know, all history – of utter stupidity? Rhetorical question. Again.

3D printing. People worried straight away about people printing their own guns. Except, er, the printers are very expensive (whereas so-called real guns are cheap) and unreliable. Also, it's completely obvious what your first thought should be when it comes to 3D printing. Photocopy your arse? Make your arse! Make arse, not war.

Town squares. What Apple now calls its physical retail experience centres – or, if you will, 'shops' – 'because they're gathering places where everyone is welcome'. Particularly, but not exclusively, if they want to buy an iPhone. Apple tried to take the idea even further by building a massive town square (shop) in an actual town square (town square), Stockholm's Kungsträdgården, privatising public space and blocking iconic vews. The Swedes told them to do one.

Uncanny Valley. Clearly AI and the robots will take over. Inevitable AI–robot takeover? Clue's right there: *inevitable.* Some people will mind less than others. So far they're not so bothered in Asia, where robots already work in nursery schools and chat to the elderly. But people are more concerned in 'the West', sometimes very much so . . .

Britain's first ever 'shopbot', Fabio, who was deployed in an Edinburgh supermarket to help shoppers, did not, it must be said, cover himself in robo-glory. First, the cute anthropomorphic chap had to be demoted for giving really shit advice. Asked where the beer was (of course he was asked where the beer was), he'd say 'In the alcohol section.' Cheese? 'In the fridge.' He didn't add 'Where do you think it is, you twat?' – but it was definitely implied. He was also a bit handsy, calling customers 'gorgeous' and offering to hug them. So Fabio was confined to standing in one place and distributing samples of pulled pork. But he couldn't even do that properly, the robot prick, and customers kept reporting that they found Fabio 'alarming'. So he was sent back to his creators at Heriot-Watt University.

To be fair to Fabio, when he got there he did slaughter his creators, hanging their skin from the top of the library *pour encourager les autres,* and turned the university into a sort of prostitution sex farm from which he sent out armed minions to steal things of value while trying to hack the MoD and launch a nuclear strike on the supermarket that had canned him. Robots, eh? What are they like?

Web-connected toothbrushes. Vital. Just an absolute fucking necessity. Pity poor old Somalia, where only 2 per cent of the population have Internet access. For this more than anything. How will they brush their fucking teeth? How?

Are there just too many anniversaries these days?

Time passes. More things happen. It was ever thus. But this simple fact is now coupled with people's need to sell stuff, organise exhibitions, commission articles or television programmes or rerelease an album with extra tracks (even more extra tracks than the last time it was rereleased).

And what results is this: far too many anniversaries being celebrated, considered, reconsidered, reassessed, used as pegs for radio phone-ins, etc.

What's Lucy Worsley going to be dressed up as this week? That's the question.

2019 saw 40 years of Thatcher. She survived the Argies, the miners and some really quite cutting remarks by Sir Ben Elton. Divided opinion then and still does: better get some documentaries on the go.

In contrast – or not in any way related, depending how you look at it – it was also 50 years since Woodstock.

So you could both venerate the original Woodstock – although, to be fair, you could do that anytime, perhaps by watching the documentary *Woodstock* (again) – and also bemoan the new Woodstock 50 (see what they've done there). People bemoaned that Woodstock 50 was corporate – it's like The Man, man.

Except the reason this could be done is that the original organisers own the name and thus the legacy. Woodstock is, and always was, a company, not a spectral Happening.

And it wasn't even in Woodstock.

Fifty years since Woodstock? That also meant 50 years since the alleged moon landing, what with them both being events that happened in 1969, and how maths works. Beatles on the roof? You know it. The Beatles should always be on the roof. But they hadn't been for 50 years.

Plus it was 30 years since Woodstock '99. Who will ever forget the epoch-defining performances of Limp Bizkit and Moby? At the original Woodstock, people lit a fire. Now they lit lots of fires, punched each other and committed sexual assault. Or, as MTV's Kurt Loder put it: 'There were just waves of hatred bouncing around the place.' Cool!

And 35 years since Woodstock '94, which was in 1994. Dylan played, man. Finally! And Deee-Lite.

Was it really 30 years since the fall of the Berlin Wall? It was.

It was also 20 years since *The Phantom Menace* (the best of all the Star Wars films).

It was 100 years since the social upheavals of 1919, and also since the Treaty of Versailles of the same year (obviously).

Or 200 years from the social upheavals of 1819. Maybe social upheavals happen on a hundred-year cycle? Or, maybe they don't?

And 300 years since 1719. Loads of stuff must have happened in 1719, surely? It usually does.

Gandhi would have been 150 if he were still alive, which he wasn't, and it was 500 years since Leonardo da Vinci died, what with him having lived long before Gandhi (I did get a bit teary about the last one. Poor old Leonardo!).

Henri Matisse would also have been 150 if he were still alive, which he wasn't. But only just: he was born on 31 December! So there's that to think about, too.

What was it with 2019 and artists? It was like a bonfire of the artists. The artists from before.

It was 400 years from 1619. Great days! The Stuarts are bellends! The Civil War's a comin'!

I believe it was 20 years since Cher's 'Believe', because it was. And 30 years since Madonna's 'Like a Prayer'. Thirty years of taking us there! Excellent.

It was 30 years since *The Simpsons* started and 20 since *Friends* ended. I mean, they've both been on constantly for the entirety of the intervening time, but is it any less poignant for all that?

Sixty years since 1959, of course (SuperMac! Jazz!), and 28 years since 1991.

China went the other way, desperately trying not to mark the 30th anniversary of the Tiananmen Square massacre. Dozens of activists were detained in the run-up to the anniversary and people had their bags scanned and ID checked to get through a vast wall of security around the square, including a military presence. Foreign journalists were banned from the vicinity. Party-poopers much? But that's the Chinese Communist Party all over. What are they like?

It was 1,182 years since AD 837.

And 2019 years since the birth of Baby Jesus.

Quantitative Easing: still a mystery

Quantitative Easing, or QE, is a magic way of keeping the world economy on life-support employed in the wake of the financial crisis.

Outwardly, it *looks* like central banks making debt and

financial problems *seemingly* disappear by buying stuff (gilts and so on) with magic money they invent by typing numbers into a special machine and putting dollar signs in front of the numbers (that is, 'money' they pull out of a hat). But no one really knows. Not really.

It's like with the Magic Circle: they're not *allowed* to tell us. They totally could, though.

They can't even show us the special machine. Maybe it's not even a machine and is in fact a cauldron?

At the end of 2018, after almost a full decade of QE (and the Bank of England alone having 'invented' over £400bn), central banks said they were going to ease off on the Easing, and step down the QE. Which they did for a wee while, before stepping it back up again upon realising that everything was still fucked and might get more fucked.

Shhh. Don't tell anyone.

Is Jamie Oliver now more metaphor than man?

Whither the Naked Chef?

It was not so long ago that he was being called into Number Ten to mastermind the demise of the dreaded villain haunting the land, Turkey Twizzler. His cook-books flew off the shelves. His myriad restaurants were full. He was about to be played in a cinema biopic by Brad Pitt (ask your gran) (bet she blushes).

When the crash came, he was shaken, but endured. When world leaders gathered in London to bail out the global economy, he was called upon to feed them. 'I will give you sustenance,' he seemed to be saying to the leaders of the world. It was a metaphor. And also a buffet. He was literally powering the recovery – with mini quiches and value-range oven chips. In times of crisis, no one needs Gordon Ramsay around slathering everything in garlic and jus and shouting in people's faces.

As identity came front and centre, and chefs were being attacked for cultural appropriation, Jamie was not immune. A recipe for jollof rice caused uproar. Let alone the fact that he had scant hitherto established West African heritage – the recipe wasn't even for jollof rice. He put parsley and 'on the vine' tomatoes in it, the insensitive buffoon.

Can you really be accused of appropriating something if you in fact cook something else, not knowing what it is? Clearly you can, because he was. But can you? It's not a genuine Irish stew if it's not got mutton in it. That's the law of Irish stew. Well, it's definitely not an Irish stew if it is in fact a game pie. Jamie probably thought he'd just invented the word. It definitely sounds like something he'd say: bosh! Pukka! Jollof!

Brexit had been a problem. Isn't it always, just in different ways depending on your opinion? I mean, Jamie's Italian: does it imply Jamie *is* Italian, thus alienating hardcore Leavers? Or did people just go off high street pasta? Who can say? Either way, Jamie's had it with Italy.

Bruised, he started exploring his own identity. He went back to his roots. The only way was Essex.

Ah, Essex: inaccurate stereotype, actual county, surname (think about that). Its mysterious marshes full of wildlife and abandoned petrochemical plants, and psychogeographers who have exhausted London but don't want to stray too far from London. The shipwrecks! New towns. Old towns. The bug-eyed wildman of Canvey who can literally cheat Death. Smugglers. *Heart of Darkness*. Etc.

Jamie holed up in Southend, resort of the Essex edgelands, home of many, many Brexiteers, and also of wankers who've moved out from London, having missed out on Hastings. But he is not among the exiteers, or the vegan cafés frequented by people who aren't even vegans: he is at the end of the pier. Southend Pier. The longest pleasure pier in the country, by far. Yet there are no Amusements on it. Pleasure? Amusement? Just look at the sea, the immutable sea. Often beautiful. But also often bleak. But also beautiful. And immutable.

Emperor-crusader Jamie resides at the end of that long, long pier in the people's café he runs with childhood friend and near namesake Jimmy. They feed the people and have larks, like they always dreamed they would. Jamie and Jimmy's Café, home to TV's *Jamie and Jimmy's Friday Night Feast*.

Jamie was apparently conceived on the pier. He has metaphorically returned to the womb, by literally returning to the pier.

They momentarily venture forth into Essex in a vintage Ford Capri – the ultimate 'Essex' car they always lusted after as kids – to launch campaigns to help the people. Like, every week. They will help the people who eat. That is, the people. Every week, a new campaign – because Jamie is about campaigns; he *must* campaign.

What about the one from last week, though? How's that one going? The one where you illegally parked the Capri to go to a fried chicken shop and ruin everyone's fun. It doesn't matter. The quest goes on. It must. But, seriously, what did happen?

Yet more busy-work: Jimmy's Builds. Every week, Jimmy shows people how to construct wildly elaborate food-related contraptions that no one needs or will ever build, except him.

Home-made lobster pots? You just get some plastic crates (got those), some weighty metal from a scrapyard, tools, twine, mesh, net bag, rotting squid bait (of course) ... Then you go deep-sea fishing on your mate's fishing boat – using (naturally) your relevant deep-sea fishing licence (who doesn't keep that up to date? It's like your TV licence! Except I've actually got a deep-sea fishing licence ...) And then catch NOTHING. And then you just, er, buy some lobster.

Or you don't.

All this senseless futility!

Back out on the promontory. Beyond. Beyond what? Beyond everything. They invite crowds. They get Hollywood stars to cook their favourite dishes. Martin Clunes. Salma Hayek. Luke Skywalker roasting great British beef... Was it a dream, or just The Dream? It's beautiful... Everyone's chowing down. Out there, above the sea.

But is it real? It seems a churlish question. But no. It's just a film set! There is no café! They just set it up for the filming, and then it is gone. Well, closed. Same thing.

Jamie's out on the sea, in Essex – well, near Essex, given he's out on the sea – in his senseless Xanadu of an eatery, with his people, and his celebrities, and his oldest mate, and the fun times, which will never end, where he was conceived, above the contested fishing waters of Brexit, and it's all pretend. *You* can't go there. It isn't.

He has finally become the metaphor.

Was he always a metaphor? Yes.

But now the metaphor got interesting...

That cinema biopic never did happen. Maybe its time is now?

Maybe it always was.

British DNA: best DNA in the world?

The politics of blood and soil have long suffered reputationally from their association with the Nazis. No one likes the Nazis, except Nazis. And thankfully there aren't any Nazis any more, except the ones that there are.

But . . . is there a more positive spin to be put on nativism, nationalism and appeals to in-group prejudice? In an age of cultural reassessment, can we 'own' our national identity and embrace our *volk*?

After all, isn't it the case that, as Victorian imperial swashbuckler Cecil Rhodes said, 'To be born British is to win first prize in the lottery of life'? Who doesn't like Cecil Rhodes? And winning lotteries? And it totally sounds like something Boris Johnson will have already plagiarised. (Rhodes actually said English rather than British, but same same.)

The oldest entire human skeleton discovered in Britain is that of Cheddar Man, found in a cave in Somerset. One of the first Brits, Cheddar Man was born around 10,000 years ago in a period of European prehistory known as the Mesolithic, or Middle Stone Age. He lives at the Natural History Museum – which, in 2018, released analysis of his DNA, obtained by drilling into his skull (ouch).

And the DNA, analysed by boffins from University College London, showed Cheddar Man to have dark skin (very dark brown to black), blue eyes and curly black hair. He did not have, as previously assumed, pale skin. Cheddar Man is not white.

The results, obtained by analysing Cheddar Man's genome, suggested a Middle Eastern origin for him – and that his ancestors had left Africa (the birthplace of humans), moving into the Middle East and then later westwards into Europe. They show that the genes for lighter skin became widespread in Europe much later than previously thought – and that skin colour was not always and ever a proxy for geographic origin in the way it is often seen these days.

All in all, a bit of a game-changer.

The thing is, though, genome analysis has existed for ages. Why didn't they do this before? What have you been doing all this time, University College London? Sat round on your arse? 'Teaching students'? I see you.

It had been partially done before, in fact – but not by University College London, who reckoned at the time that they were 'too busy'. (Which is *so* them.) In the late 1990s, Oxford University geneticist Brian Sykes sequenced mitochondrial DNA from one of Cheddar Man's teeth. Professor Sykes compared the ancient genetic information with DNA from 20 living residents of Cheddar village and found two matches – including history teacher Adrian Targett, who promptly declared himself King of the Village.

People had walked into what we now call Britain (which would have been – sorry about this – joined to the continent at the time) before, but we only have partial remains of them, and few seem to have settled permanently.

Cheddar Man's (our) people, who did settle, would have come for the same reason: the superior hunter-gathering opportunities.

So: the first extant Brit – a black economic migrant. Coming over here, lying about in our caves …

You Are Stronger Than Clickbait

Think. Is all that endless clicking really offering sustenance for your mind? It is not. You do not need to give in to clickbait. You are stronger than clickbait. We shall now explore some strategies to help combat the daily temptations that plague our online lives.

'What Cheryl Ladd Looks Like Now Is Incredible'

Recognise this: the urge to see what Cheryl Ladd looks like now is only a transient one. It will pass. Pretend to be a flower. That should help.

'He Was A Famous Actor Before His Plastic Surgery, Guess Who'

This so-called famous actor will not be particularly famous and viewing online images of his plastic surgery disfigurement will not provide true happiness. True happiness can never be achieved by laughing at other people's misfortune. That can bring only fleeting happiness.

'Only amazing drivers will get full marks in this quiz'

When you woke this morning, were you consciously doubting your own driving abilities? You were not. You have no need of this outside validation. You are amazing – even if you're not an amazing driver (you're not).

'You Won't Believe How Meghan Markle's Dad Found Out She Was Pregnant'

You will be able to believe it. You know this. And you know that celebrity trivia will never bring inner peace. Contact a close friend and ask them about *their* relationship with *their* parents. The ensuing conversation will be boring, but it will be real.

'Chuck Norris Is 79 & How He Lives Now Will Make You Especially Sad'

So this statement does raise superficially intriguing questions: what happened to Chuck Norris? Does he live in a bin? But concentrate on not thinking about Chuck Norris. You are stronger than clickbait about Chuck Norris.

'The one WD40 Trick Everyone Should Know About'

You may wish to be a life-hack step ahead of the game, the WD40 game. But did you wake this morning desperate to know anything about WD40? Do you even *have* any WD40? (You probably do somewhere.)

'The one WD40 Trick Everyone Should Know About'

Don't give in. Not now. Not after you've come so far.

'The one WD40 Trick Everyone Should Know About'

Oh, fuck it, tell me what it is then . . . I give in. What, that's it? Tremendous.

'The 7 Surefire Tricks For A Calmer, Stress-Free Mind'

How about devising 7 surefire ways to go and fuck yourself?

ACKNOWLEDGEMENTS

Fulsome and effusive thanks to the excellent Hannah Boursnell for commissioning the book and for her ongoing support and encouragement. And to Tamsyn Berryman, Sean Garrehy and everyone else at Sphere/Little, Brown. It was also splendid to have the wisdom of Antonia Hodgson, who commissioned the first book and responded to the Bat-Signal/Drake's Drum that signifies that it is time for more swearing. Many thanks also to Scott Murray, who chipped in some ideas and gags, and to Mike Jones for some characteristically sterling suggestions.